A ROMANY A

2012.

To Dad
    Merry Christmas &A Happy
    New Year.
       Love
       Ginny, Cliff, Thomas & William,
         × × × ×

A
ROMANY AND RAQ

THE ROMANY
OF THE B.B.C.
(G. BRAMWELL EVENS)

With Illustrations by the Author

ISIS
LARGE PRINT
Oxford

First published in Great Britain 1930
by The Epworth Press

Published in Large Print 2003 by ISIS Publishing Ltd,
7 Centremead, Osney Mead, Oxford OX2 0ES
by arrangement with Mrs Romany Watts

British Library Cataloguing in Publication Data
Evens, George Bramwell
    A Romany and Raq. – Large print ed. –
(Isis reminiscence series)
    1. Natural history – Great Britain
    2. Large type books
    I Title
    508.4'1

ISBN 0–7531–9836–3 (hb)
ISBN 0–7531–9837–1 (pb)

Printed and bound by Antony Rowe, Chippenham

"*Give me the clear blue sky over my head
   and the green turf beneath my feet
a winding road before me . . .
   and then to thinking.*"

TO MY GIPSY MOTHER
WHO GAVE ME MY LOVE OF
GREEN FIELDS AND QUIET LANES

CONTENTS

A ROMANY AND RAQ

in which we re-introduce you to

JOHN FELL	*Gamekeeper*
JERRY	*Poacher*
ALAN AND JOE	*Farmers*
NED	*Village Postman*
JOHN RUBB	*Angler*
SALLY STORDY	*Cottager*

CHAPTER
ONE

The Lure of the Open Air

AUGUST

I do not remember a time when the countryside had no fascination for me. Give me a lane and a hedge, and heaven lies in exploring its shadows and becoming intimate with its shy inhabitants. Probably this is due to the fact that I spring from pure gipsy stock. In my veins runs the blood of nomads who have sought the solitudes for hundreds of centuries. It is this ancestry which has made me a roamer, and like a bird hearing its migratory call, so the fields and the woods lure me from city life.

I know what it is to climb the stiff cliffs of lonely Ailsa Craig, to listen to the chant of the gannets as I photographed them on the narrow ledges which overlooked the sea four hundred feet below. I can hear again the cry of the kittiwakes and oystercatchers as I neared their nests on other lonely islands of the Scottish coasts. Yet of all the places I have visited, there is none which yields me so much content as rambling round the countryside.

★   ★   ★

Could you take a peep at my caravan, where it now rests, you would see it shadowed by boughs on which the apples lie thickly and heavily. By the side of it runs a hedge where the bees lumber cumbrously on to the bramble blossom, and where the "lintie" sings a plaintive litany as she sways on some slender bough.

Just behind the tents runs the stream. I can hear its tiny tinkle even as I write. A very subdued yet high melody it is singing — the melody of a thin string, of shallow waters, of attenuated channels. All its dryads and nymphs are for the moment tremulous sopranos.

But the hoped-for rain will come ere long and the tone will change. The ringing of its bells will give place to a roar and hiss of triumph. Then from their lairs will issue forth the big trout. Up from the neighbouring river the sea-trout will seek its yellow waters, thirsting for the flavour of the beck which perchance first gave them birth.

★   ★   ★

My caravan has a history. It has rumbled along the roads and lanes and heard the chatter of the Romanies as the light of the camp-fire lit up their swarthy faces. I am reminded of them by the big box attached to the rear. This big receptacle was most useful when passing turnip or potato fields — not to put many in at once, that was not necessary, for there were plenty of other fields to be passed, and the box would still be there!

That hook on the axle is where Boz, the lurcher, was tethered, and under which, when any strangers were about, he used to lie as meek as a lamb. In their presence, he cultivated a slight limp and had the knack of looking prematurely old. But as soon as their backs were turned, a rejuvenated Phoenix would have looked antiquated beside him, especially as he "sleuthed" it up the hedgeside.

The hook is still behind the van, but the lurcher that never barked, and never knew when he was beaten, is now in other happy hunting grounds, R.I.P.

★ ★ ★

As I lounge by the caravan steps a flash of green and scarlet streaks through the trees, dodging the trunks with marvellous precision. Then from the end of the orchard there comes a joyous "yaffle." It holds in its tone satisfaction and derision. I listen for a moment and then hear a definite strong tapping of the wood. It is the green wood-pecker, at work. He owns the orchard too. When, in the thousands of years that have rolled by, his ancestors determined to seek their living on the barks of trees, with occasional relapses in the direction of ant-hills and marshy ground, Nature fashioned their bodies to suit their habits.

The All-Mother has been very generous to him and his kind. She has made him a specialist in the art of

probing. His bill is a strong drill. From where I sit I can see him driving at the tree-trunk. I cannot see the individual drives, so fast does he withdraw and strike, withdraw and strike. All I can see is a blur of green and cardinal. Then I can hear the reverberating thuds.

Could I crawl nearer I should see that his tail is very different from that of the sparrow chirping from the caravan roof. Indeed he uses it almost as a stool, and, pressing it firmly against the bark, sits on it. With his two feet such an arrangement makes an excellent tripod stand. Steadied thus he searches with his long telescopic tongue for the hiders in the bark.

I would like you to see that tongue, for on the end of it is a barb such as you find on an angler's hook. Feel it, and you will notice that Nature has dipped it in seccotine. It is a harpoon for the struggling larvae and the stickiness picks up the smallest of fry.

Look! he is — but the bird has caught my slightest movement, and with a derisive chuckle is lost in the neighbouring trees.

★　★　★

When night draws down her curtain on the orchard in which the caravan rests, then the fire is lit. With Raq my constant companion, a spaniel with an animal's sensitiveness and a human being's understanding, I sit and watch the pine logs flicker. The incense rises, and as the smoke curls upwards into indigo night, I see the faces of those who love the countryside as I do and interpret its phases to me.

Away up in the fields I hear the call of the ewes to their lambs and my mind flies at once to the farm where Alan and Joe live. What hospitality Joe's wife and the sisters offer to me! How great is their never varying welcome.

Then the silence is broken by the bark of a fox, and in spirit I am with John Fell, the gamekeeper. That bark, I know, will make him uneasy about the safety of his young pheasants, and I can see him walking round his sanctuary in the hope of heading off the sleuth of the woods. Soon, from the stream behind me, I hear the plunge of a sea-trout, and I wonder whether my friend John Rubb, is bringing any to their doom by his skilful casting of the "fly."

I think also of Jerry, the poacher, but not a "ne'er do well." I marvel at the queer nature of the man which endears him to all who know him — even the keeper is one of his friends. As I think of him I envy, too, the rich store of knowledge which he has of every bird and beast. I envy him, too, his lovely thatched cottage which nestles on the fringe of a wood. Musing thus, I feel how blessed I am in my friends. Who would not delight to go with Ned, the village postman, as he delivers his letters to distant farms, and to listen to him as he unfolds the marvels of insect, flower or pond life? Then there is Sally Stordy whose cottage is a refuge and a rest, and whose quaint outlook on life and her sound common sense is a joy to listen to.

I love the smithy, too. To begin with, it has a smell all its own. The byre has its own fragrance; so has the barn. No one can mistake the floury dry mustiness of the granary. But the smithy is a mixture of burning horn and scorching leather.

Of course, the blacksmith has his work to do, and does it well. But what the shop and post-office are to the women of the village, the smithy is to the men-folk. It is the unofficial B.B.C. of the district.

There is, too, an air of timelessness about its smoke-grimed walls, and here and there are unconventional seats worn smooth and bright by the corduroys of its habitués. Talk flares up at intervals, even as the bellows call on the slumbering fire to wake up and glow red, and the smith, even though he be beating out a merry tattoo on the anvil, still manages to catch the spicy tit-bits of gossip as newcomers drop in and range themselves amongst the shadows.

At the village shop, smoke seen issuing from an unused chimney is sufficient to keep the ball of gossip rolling for a whole morning. Who knows but what it may portend the arrival of a visitor, or perchance that fire burning through the night may mean that a new bairn has arrived. The absence of the usual smoke from Sally Stordy's washhouse will call forth a torrent of questions as to the reason for this departure from the usual.

But in the smithy runs the rumour of a new kind of threshing-machine which Dick Pennington is getting, or men speak in admiration of the price which Jim Sheppard received for his lambs.

As the darkness deepens in the orchard then the bat swings round and round in uneven undulating circles. Above the top of the grass the white moths are doing the ghost dance. The owl leaves the warm barn, and after sitting motionless on some bare branch sweeps down with deadly precision towards the darkening grass.

The stars are out and the last pale shimmer of light shows from the top of the hills. I go towards the tent and throw myself on the bed. I can see the Pole Star and Great Bear blinking at me through the open flap. The hayrick sends to me its final benediction. The world is drowsy, only a young cockerel mistakes the hour and begins to crow prematurely.

Now, too, the brook is singing its sweetest lullaby. A distant train I can hear rushing to some town where poor folks are sleeping in stuffy rooms whilst I am bathed in the wonders of a velvet world. Ah, well! I must turn in.

CHAPTER
TWO

Market-Day

APRIL

How varied is Nature's wardrobe. Last week it wore an ermine cloak, Raq and I now found a smiling landscape before us, with the catkins quivering in the sunlight and the bluebells pushing their green spikes upwards.

In nearly every field we saw the dark head of a partridge raised. A couple of mated birds whirred their way into a neighbouring field, from which, within a moment or two, we heard the sound of bickering and combat. To avoid us the pair had had to trespass on the territory of another couple, and male would spar with male, and even the demure hen would square up to another of her own sex. Very little harm would be done. Probably it was one way of working off the spring ardour.

Ned, the old postman, found me gazing intently into a pond that nestled in a clump of trees.

"Those are not fish moving about in the water, are they?" I asked, pointing to the centre of the pond where the surface was continually being ruffled, as though a small shoal of mackerel were darting about.

8

Ned shook his head. "It's the trystin' place o' the frogs," he said simply.

I looked at him, and waited for his explanation.

"All through t' winter," he continued, "them frogs 'as bin hibernatin'. Have ye ever found any?"

I shook my head.

"Sometimes," said Ned, "they lie in holes singly. Sometimes a whole heap on 'em 'll flatten 'emselves together as though they were huddlin' up fer warmth. Mind ye, ye can't feel they're warm. They're aboot as warm in yer 'ands as cold mutton. But inside 'em are stores o' fat, and they comes oot of their winter sleep ready fer spawnin'. That's a miracle a'most in itsen."

He looked at me to see if I understood what he was saying.

"You mean," I said, "that they ought to be too thin and exhausted after their winter sleep to think of laying eggs, and so using up what strength they had left?"

"That's it noo," said Ned appreciatively in a tone which a schoolmaster would use to some scholar who was making satisfactory progress. "Well," he went on, "as soon as they wak' up, they set off fer some pond or ditch. They know where it is and mak' a bee-line fer 't. Some ponds they won't have at no price — they pass by 'em. This pond here doesn't look very invitin' to you and me. But ever sin I were a boy ye could allus find it full o' 'em, and I reckon they've bin comin' to it p'raps fer 'undreds and 'undreds o' years."

★ ★ ★

Not far from the village we met Sally Stordy, with a large basket on her arm, the contents covered with a spotless linen cloth.

Raq sniffed at it with approval, and I heard Sally say, "Ye'd like some o' that butter in there, I reckon, wouldn't ye, old fellow?"

Ned went off on his rounds when he saw me taking the heavy weight from Sally.

Then I asked her where she was going.

"I'm just off to market," she said. "Whiterigg's missus isn't just up to t' mark, so I'm takin' her butter and eggs to Penworth fer 'er."

"I'll go with you, Sally," I said, suddenly changing my plans. "Are you making for the station?"

She shook her head. "My car and 'shuvver' are at t' bottom o' t' hill," she said smilingly, and then I remembered that the 'bus ran past the crossroads.

As we waited for it, a number of cars flashed by, all packed with baskets similar to the one set down at my side. Sally seemed to know all the drivers.

10

"It used to be carrier's cart fer that lot," said Sally, nodding in the direction taken by the cars, "only a few years sin. The driver o' t' last un were Tom Hutchinson. He never thowt he'd run his own car when 'e were a lad. His father started like our Tom, wi' only a few shillin's a week and eight childer, and his father afore 'im were nowt. But 'e's got on, I reckon. He's a hard un, but a worker, mind ye."

Then an old-fashioned "gig" ambled by. How quaint they looked perched up in back-to-back seats. Sticking up by the side of the baskets which were stowed in the back I caught a glimpse of one of those large umbrellas under which the occupants used to hide in bad weather.

"There's no need fer Tom Graham to drive that owd mare," said Sally, after it had passed. "It's gone to market every week fer twenty years, an' could go there blindfold. He's a near un is Tom. That's his owd missus sittin' by 'im. She's wore that black bonnet wi' a yaller flower on 't fer ower fifteen years to my knowledge, and when she goes to a funeral she tak's flower off and —"

Then the 'bus — crowded with farmers and their wives, dealers, buyers — came snorting along, and picking up the dog in my arms, we managed to stow ourselves amongst the multitudinous baskets which occupied every available inch of space.

★ ★ ★

I left Sally at the "Royal George," where the 'bus stopped, telling her that I should probably find her in the market later on.

The little town of Penworth was alive. For six days in the week it lies in a comatose condition, but on market-day it really wakes up. I walked to the centre, where stands the cross, and around which is a good-sized square. Here are displayed ploughs, separators, troughs, spades, fertilizers, and a hundred other things which a farm demands.

Round about these I could see scores of men, and as I wanted to find Alan and Joe, my farmer friends, I

walked amongst them.

As I passed one little group, I felt my arm pulled, and the next moment I was in a circle of men amongst whom were my two friends. None of them resented my presence. Some of them nodded gravely at me.

First of all I found myself listening to a language that was entirely foreign. Men were talking about "grey-faced lambing hoggs," "wether hoggs," "shearlings," "brood mares."

I looked hopelessly at Alan, and he whispered that he would explain later. So I took the opportunity of observing our neighbours. All were gathered in groups similar to my own. Each group was in a constant state of flux. Men were continually sidling into it. Others were continually abstracting themselves and moving on to fresh circles. Neither handshakes nor introductions were indulged in.

How delightfully different from the formal conventionalities of town!

Sometimes the group discussed prices. Then a bit of gossip would be related. Then a name would be mentioned, and sometimes men shook their heads as they heard it, or looked away up the street as they spoke it. The group understood these signs, and knew just what such mannerisms were meant to convey.

I think that it would take each man three or four hours to revolve all the way round the square. But in those three hours how much knowledge could be absorbed! And the things learnt would then be carried to remote hamlets, and to still more remote farmsteads.

"Not many best hoggs aboot," said a farmer to me, and I saw Joe looking at me wondering what I should answer.

"Not many," I replied, trying to look as though I understood what he was talking about.

"Stirks are fetchin' aboot fifteen pun," he continued, giving me a quizzical look.

"A very useful price," I said knowingly, and I could see Alan and Joe nudging one another and almost bursting with laughter at my non-committal answer.

"That's the word to use when ye're in doot," said Alan to me later. "There's nowt like words such as 'fairish,' 'goodish,' and 'useful.' If ye'd a said 'splendid' he'd a know'd ye were a townsman."

⋆ ⋆ ⋆

I wandered into the market. Before me ran long rows of tables scrubbed white. Each table had a number on it. Here, with their baskets full of farm produce, stood the farmers' wives. Customers moved up and down those long rows, examining chickens, feeling rabbits, scrutinizing eggs, and asking questions.

I found Sally standing by her wares, and a little later she left me, to speak to a friend.

Just at that moment a hard-featured woman came up. Only for a fleeting second did she glance at me. Then, down went her head towards the eggs in Sally's basket, as though she were judging them by the smell.

"What are the eggs?" she rapped out like a drill-sergeant.

I was rather taken aback by this onslaught. I have in my short lifetime been taken for many things — poacher, parson, solicitor, and commercial traveller — but I had never yet been mistaken for a purveyor of farmyard commodities. I look too simple for that.

However, I rose to the occasion, and after swallowing hard, I replied professionally. "These," pointing to the brown ones, "are laid by Rhode Island Reds, whilst these" (here I put my finger on the white ones) "are produced by White Leg —"

"Naw," my customer broke in scornfully, "how much are ye askin'?"

14

"One and five a dozen," I promptly replied.

"Ye'll ha' to come doon a bit, I reckon," she replied, as she walked away.

Later I saw her examining other baskets, and I followed my almost-customer at a respectful distance. Right down the long lanes of selling humanity she cruised. How many times she stopped before a basket and smelled the eggs, how many times she stopped and asked the same question as she had asked me, I cannot say. After the tenth time I lost sight of her.

Probably, somewhere or other, she finally found some anxious vendor and got a dozen eggs for one and four. In talking to her neighbours, she would probably gloat over the fact that she had bought eggs at a penny cheaper than they had done. That would be her moment of triumph. She would be known as a keen buyer.

But if she had sat down quietly and reckoned up carefully, she would have found that in saving a penny on eggs, she had probably worn out three-pennyworth of shoe-leather. That is the worst of having an economical mind!

★　★　★

I told Sally of my experience, and she laughed heartily. "That calls to my mind summat that happened once," she said. "A woman came roond and looked at my basket, which was full o' eggs. 'I want a dozen eggs,' she said, 'that 'ave bin laid by black hens.' Well, I didn't know which had bin laid by black or which had bin laid by white 'uns, but I told her to pick 'er own if she knew t' diff'rence atween 'em. Can you tell the diff'rence?" Sally asked me.

I shook my head. "I don't believe anyone can," I said.

"Well," said Sally, with a grim smile, "she could. She turned ower the eggs and began puttin' 'em in 'er basket, and when she'd got 'er dozen she said, 'Them are a'reet.' As she paid me for 'em I said to 'er, lookin' at the eggs, 'It seems to me that black hens lay all the biggest eggs.' 'Aye,' she said as she turned away, 'that's 'ow ye tell 'em.'"

★   ★   ★

I, too, made a purchase, for, by the side of one basket lay a tiny bunch of primroses. How my heart rejoiced when I saw them! They had been gathered from some quiet nook where the keen wind could not penetrate. From their snug retreat they had caught every ray of the sun, and now smiled them back at me.

I bought them and felt sorry for them. Although I delighted in them, yet I would ten thousand times rather have found them myself, and so have enjoyed their simple beauty in their natural setting.

They now rest in a tiny vase on my mantelpiece. Outside a cold wind is blowing, and dark clouds are gathering. But these little flowers are the "earnest of our inheritance."

CHAPTER
THREE

On Hiding Things

APRIL

How different the woods are in spring from winter! I do not mean that they appear so different, but feel different. Only a few months ago there was the sense of damp deadness. Now, there is the thrill of vibrant life.

Where the rotting leaves lay sombre and dull, to-day the spikes of the bluebells are pushing upwards, and the little wood anemones shiver with delighted ecstasy. Even the barks of the trees look fresh. The silver birch shimmers in the April sun, whilst the trunks of the great beech trees look sleek, well-groomed, and in certain lights, are touched with the sheen of silver and pale lavender.

I found Raq interested in something which lay buried in the mould. It was a hen which lay completely covered save for a feather or two which swayed in the light breeze.

"Now what's done that?" I said to the dog, and I noticed that he was casting around for some telltale scent. He found it and knew what it was, for the hair round his throat was slightly raised, which boded ill for the owner of the trail.

"What is it?" I asked of the dog, as he looked at me with intelligent eyes.

"A fox, I should say," said a deep voice behind me, and rather startled by the suddenness of it, I turned and saw Jerry.

"You did give me a start," said I. "Neither I nor the dog knew you were about."

The old poacher laughed at this tribute to his quietness of movement.

"That's the work of a fox," he said.

"Or a cat that's taken to the woods," I suggested.

Jerry shook his head. "As a rule a cat don't bury and leave tell-tale traces of his work like them feathers stickin' oot, and he don't scratch a hole like that generally. An old Tom covers anythin' he wants to hide, rather than buries. Pulls ower it moss and leaves, but doesn't dig a grave — leastways that's my experience on 'em."

"But I thought a fox would be too cunning to leave such traces of his foraging?" I said.

"No," answered my friend; "that's the funny part on't. He's cunnin' enough to find an entrance into a fowl-house, and fool enough to let his larder betray him. Funny how most criminals, they tell me, allus leave behind 'em a clue o' some sort, which shows up their stupidness rather than their smartness."

As we passed on together through the wood I asked what he had been doing, and for answer he pulled out of his capacious inner pocket a half-a-dozen good-sized trout.

"And were they rising well?" I asked, knowing the weather to be on the cold side, and the hatch of flies to be rather scanty.

"Only when I made 'em," said he with a chuckle. "I brought 'em oot o' their hidin'-places right enough."

"And where's your tackle — rod and line?" I asked severely.

"Here," he said gayly, rolling back his sleeve and displaying a discoloured arm, with hand and fingers working dexterously.

"You've been tickling them then?" I asked.

He nodded. "Old Nancy Fairbairn up yonder, her that's bin so bad wi' rheumaticks, said she fancied a nice fresh trout. So I browned me arm wi' mud and went doon to the beck where it meets the river, and guddled fer 'em."

"Is it easy to get them like that?" I asked.

"Easy as eatin' butter," he said, "if ye only know 'ow. Ye work 'em under a big stone or overhangin' bank; then doon goes yer arm, and ye feel fer 'em wi' yer fingers — then oot wi' 'em."

"And how do you know when to grip them?" I asked.

"You tickle 'em until ye hear 'em laugh," said the old vagabond joyously. "Or snore," he added, giving me a poke somewhere in the region of my ribs.

★   ★   ★

Near the edge of the wood the dog chased a squirrel, which leapt for safety up the trunk of a pine.

I called him to heel, whilst I craned my neck upwards to see whether I could locate him in the topmost branches.

"He ain't there," whispered Jerry, pointing towards the high branches.

"How do you know?" I asked. "Can you see him?"

Jerry shook his head. "Follow the lead o' yer dog's nose, and ye'll find that he's only aboot four feet up the trunk on the side furthest from us. He knows ye'll be looking fer 'im high up, so he keeps low down — they allus do."

Jerry moved cautiously a few feet to my right, and immediately "Brighteyes" sped up the tree to the nearest fork. Here he chattered at us and hurled down every epithet of abuse for disturbing his search for a morning meal.

"His language is quite sq-irreligious," said Jerry, with a grin, and it was my turn this time to poke him in the ribs for making such an outrageous pun.

"Let's sit doon and watch him for a few minutes," said he. "But come here first," and pointing at the fork of a big holly-bush, he added, "I'll wager anythin' ye like that that's where the little beggar's 'drey' is."

"Drey?" I repeated.

"Nest," my friend interpreted.

And so we sat down some distance from the pine from which the squirrel still looked down on us, and waited for him to reveal himself further.

★ ★ ★

As we sat there quietly, Jerry talked in low tones. "That there fox we was talkin' aboot just now 'as somethin' in common even wi' yon little bushytail."

"Yes?" I said, so hesitatingly that my friend knew that it was an invitation to explain further.

"The squirrel hides things too, but not in the same way as the fox. And though he doesn't kill birds and bury 'em carelessly, he's just as 'ap'azard in what he does bury."

"You are referring to his habit of laying up stores for the winter, and then hibernating?" I suggested.

"Well," said my friend, "in a way, yes! But first of all, don't run away with the idee that a squirrel 'ibernates — he doesn't, though that's what the books'll tell ye. He sartainly 'as more'n forty winks in winter, but I've seen him scamperin' aboot the trees when there's bin a foot o' snow on t' groond."

"But he lays up stores of food for himself, for I've found them," I persisted.

"It's not the stores which he 'ides that I'm a thinkin' on," said Jerry, "but if ye watch him when the nuts, hazel and acorns is ripe, then ye'll see him dart to some bank, or trip ower to some barren bit o' groond, and after scrapin' a hole, shove a nut in. Then he carefully scrats and covers it. He'll do dozens and dozens like that."

Jerry indicated how the little chap carried the nut by putting his own tongue in the side of his cheek. "This is his pouch," he explained.

"And can he remember all these hidden and separate treasures?" I asked.

"Not 'im," said Jerry decisively. "That's my point. Where the fox is careless in his hiding, old 'Bushy-tail' is fergitful in his buryin's. And the result?" Here the old poacher turned to me for the answer.

"He has to fall back on his main stores?" I answered.

"That's not the answer I wanted," said Jerry. "The result is a far bigger thing than merely fillin' a squirrel's inside. The result is" — here he paused to emphasize his remark — "an ever more beautiful world."

To say that I was perplexed is to put it mildly.

"However can the production of beauty be linked up with a squirrel's forgetfulness?" So ran my thoughts, and Jerry simply watched me, laughing in his own hearty way.

Seeing that I could not answer his riddle, he said —

"Well, now, what happens to the fergotten nut or the hidden seed?" Jerry answered his own question. "Natur' doesn't fergit it. Mother Earth holds it in her arms, and the rain in due course softens it, and the sun kisses it into new life. And lo! where no trees grew, up comes the oak, the beech, and the hazel. The squirrel 'as become one o' God's unpaid gardeners. He's an unknowin' sower o' beauty, and so it's a good thing to have a bad mem'ry sometimes, eh?"

★ ★ ★

A few minutes later our little friend in the pine fork had lost a good deal of his shyness. He treated us to a wonderful display of gymnastics. Along a strong branch he raced. Without any hesitation he launched himself on to a gracefully drooping beech. Under his weight the branch hardly swayed, and so perfect was the jump that the little gymnast hardly seemed to pause in his stride.

On the beech tree he found another squirrel, which we had not seen. Evidently the second one had been watching us, and the first squirrel had spotted him, and as soon as he had recovered his pluck, had sprung to meet him.

Up and down they sped. Sometimes they seemed to close in combat. Sometimes I thought it was but a game of chase.

"He's driving him out of his own territory," said Jerry to me. "That second feller had no right in that there tree, and 'e knows it."

"So the squirrels, as well as the birds, stake out their claim to certain trees, do they?" I asked.

Jerry nodded. "The second chap, he'll have a selected tree or two, which he marks, 'Private — No

Road.' And 'atween 'is little park and our first friend's, there'll be a sort o' 'No Man's Land,' where very often the two on 'em'll fraternize and pass the time o' day, and even play. But it's war if one swings on to the bough claimed by another."

★   ★   ★

As I walked homewards I kept thinking of the squirrel that rushed its neighbour out of its own domain. It would not have harmed the little beggar to have allowed him to stay.

Everywhere in the wild there seems to be this claim for Private Property. There is little sharing. All are out to hold what they have got.

Possibly the newcomer might have been a raider, and might have robbed his neighbour of a store of nuts and acorns — therefore he had to be headed off.

The squirrel claims his trees, the thrush and robin guard their gardens, the big trout holds his favourite position in the river against all comers. Even the dipper preserves her part of the stream and the otter allows no intruders. But what they guard is their food supply — their vital necessities.

Then I looked up at a beautiful wood, and on it was "Trespassers will be prosecuted." But that was put up by a landowner. The squirrel's instinct has evidently been handed down to us!

CHAPTER
FOUR

Nature's Safeguards

APRIL

We met John Fell the gamekeeper on the fringe of the wood. He was carrying a small spade. His gun rested over his shoulder, whilst over his back was slung a bag in which were a couple of small rabbit-nets. In another smaller bag of canvas was a ferret, whose frequent scratchings showed that it wished to be free.

"Just gettin' a few odd rabbits that are damaging some young trees," John said by way of explanation, for he knew how I hated a gun.

Raq and I joined him, and as we walked along kept our eyes open for likely burrows.

"There's a likely one here," I said, stopping in front of one.

John looked at it for a moment, shook his head, and passed on.

"What's wrong with it?" I asked, just a trifle annoyed that he had given it such scanty attention.

"The veil's on it," he answered, and seeing that I did not understand what he meant, turned back, and we viewed the hole together.

"Look carefully," he said.

Then I saw that some tiny spider had stretched three silken tight-ropes across the entrance. From a certain angle they glistened with the night's frost.

"No need to try any burrow when that little curtain is there," said the keeper. "Saves a 'eap o' time and trouble if yer keep yer eyes skinned."

Further on Raq stood before a similar entrance.

"There's a rabbit in there," I said decisively.

"Sure?" asked my companion.

"Dead sure," I answered, and as John forbore to ask how I knew, I proceeded to tell him.

"When Raq finds a hole he always smells at it. If it's empty, he gives one sniff and turns away, though his tail works on as usual. But if there's a rabbit in it, he gives a second long in-drawn smell, and for a moment that wagging pendulum stands out straight in a line with his back, stiff as a poker; then it nearly wags itself off his body. Look at it now."

"We'll prove it," said John, and, as I called the dog off, he put the ferret in.

The little hunter paused for a second, shook itself, and then, with a slow shuffling gait, disappeared into the darkness.

A silence fell on our little group. The keeper's well-worn gun-barrels gleamed wickedly in the sunshine; Raq, tense and expectant, concentrated every faculty on the place from which he expected "Bunny" to bolt; from the heart of the wood a ring-dove cooed out smooth love to his mate. Then a scuffle sounded in the burrow and a light fawn wraith dashed into the open. An ear-splitting crash cut short the love-song of the dove, a tiny wisp of blue smoke floated from the right-hand barrel of the gun, and Raq was returning with a little limp body in his mouth.

"Good dorg," said John, patting the dog as he received the rabbit.

I turned away. Death was out of place in that quiet sanctuary.

★ ★ ★

A moment later the ferret appeared at the "bolt" from which the rabbit had raced. He wore an aggrieved expression.

"Good worker?" I asked. The keeper picked him up in the only safe way, thumb and forefinger round the supple neck.

"Not so good as I 'ave 'ad," said John, and judging by the way he said it that a reminiscence was not very far away, I waited for him to continue.

"Best ferret I ever 'ad was a cross between it and a stoat."

"Easy to handle?" I queried.

John shook his head with a grim smile.

"He was cussedness itself," he said, and pointed to a couple of small scars on his fingers. "Them's his visitin'-cards that he left behind."

"How did you come by him?" I asked.

"Lost a little bitch-ferret whilst we were clearing out a burrow," he explained. "We dug fer 'er, but couldn't find 'er nohow. I came across 'er about six weeks later, and when 'er young 'uns arrived we found they were half-stoat, half-ferret."

John glanced at his marked fingers again and said —

"But they did me a good turn, all the same."

I looked at him inquiringly, and he went on with his story.

"There was a feller, a farmer, that was allus borrowin' my ferrets. Now I don't mind doin' a chap a good turn, but he wasn't very perticler 'ow he handled 'em. So when he come up to me one mornin' and said 'Can you lend me a ferret this mornin', John?' I 'anded him one of the cross-breeds, at the same time tellin' him to be careful in usin' it."

"What happened?" I asked.

"I can't say exactly," answered the keeper slowly, "but next mornin' he 'anded it back to me without a word o' thanks. But I noticed that three of 'is fingers had bandages on, and on the Saturday 'is wife took more young chickens and ducklin's to market than iver she'd carried in her mortal life."

"Had the ferret got out in the night and — ?" I asked.

"I'm not sayin' what 'appened," said John, with a smile. "I'm only tellin' ye the facts. But he never borrered any more o' my ferrets."

"John," I said, "if a ferret mates up with a stoat, why doesn't a chaffinch link up with a goldfinch, or a blackbird with a thrush? Why do the different species of animals keep themselves to themselves? Does the rabbit look at the hare and say, 'The Jews have no dealings with the Samaritans'?"

"In other words," said John slowly, "Why isn't there a general mix-up amongst Natur's children — donkeys with horns on, pigeons with a sparrerhawk's talons, pike with the silver scales of a salmon, eh?"

"That's what I mean," I said. "You never come across an animal half-dog and half-cat."

"Well," said John, "to begin with, it's again Natur'. Have you ever seen a cage-bird that's called a 'mule'?" he asked.

"Half-canary and half-linnet," I said.

"Aye, that's it," answered he. "There's a bit o' compulsion about their matin' up which never happens when they're wild. But," he added, "ye never found a 'mule' yet that ever 'ad a nest and eggs of its own, did yer?"

"No," I answered thoughtfully, "I don't think I ever did."

"That's 'ow Natur' puts a stop to tricks o' that kind," said the keeper. "Man by his jugglin' may produce a freak. But that freak has no power to bring into the world a whole succession o' freaks — it dies, and the race goes on pure."

★　★　★

As we ambled our way through the wood, John turned to me and said —

"Like to see an early nest?"

He took my answer for granted, and led the way to a rock bank. There on a ledge, dry and secluded, lay the home of a thrush.

"Mud-lined as usual," I said, and I looked at the four young birds, which were packed tight in its comfortable circle.

"Mud and summat else," said the keeper.

"What's the summat else?" I asked.

"What you call saliva and what I call 'spit,'" said John, suiting the action to the word. "It makes the cheapest and best o' linoleums — wish I knew how to prodooce it."

The youngsters, with no lesson of fear instilled into them, raised themselves and opened capacious mouths.

"As soon as a parson appears they're ready to 'take the collection,' you see," said John facetiously. "See the yeller line that sets off the outside o' their mouths?"

"I do," I answered, "it makes an effective colour scheme with the bright scarlet of their throats."

"That's what it's meant to do, I reckon," said my companion appreciatively. "Them yeller stripes are time and laber-savers."

I looked at him for an interpretation.

"Well, you see," he explained, "the parent-birds are kept pretty busy, and most nests are in the shadder of a bush where the light's none too good. So Natur' provides 'em with an illuminated sign, and the yeller gleams out in the darkness, cryin' out, 'Yer needn't waste time findin' the ever-open door — it's lit up fer ye — just drop the grub inside the shining line.'"

30

We watched from a safe distance the coming of the mother bird. She gave a short staccato call. Four snuggling youngsters immediately raised their heads, and a chorus of expectant squeaks proceeded from them. A short flight of the thrush, a moment of consideration as she gazed at her charges, a quick dip of the head into one red gullet, a speedy swallow by the lucky recipient, and she was away again, followed by rallentando disappointed cries of those unfed.

As we tramped on I turned to John and said —

"What's to prevent the sisters and brothers of one nest mating up together and so thinning the blood of the race? They have no laws, no tables of affinity warning them against it. If cross-breeding is prevented by Nature, what about in-breeding?"

John considered for a while, and then said —

"In-breeding, speakin' generally, is a bad thing, and Natur' knows it. Fer downright grit, hardness and common-sense, a good mongrel will often lick a thoroughbred into fits."

"I agree," I said; "there was old Boz that belonged to my grandfather —"

But I saw that John showed impatience at what he thought might be a long yarn, and my tide of reminiscence ebbed out.

"A truly wunnerful thing will happen to them young birds," he continued, as my flow suddenly ceased. "Those youngsters will be flyin' in about three weeks."

He looked at me to see whether I was nettled at being choked off my story, but seeing only interest, he patted me on the back with his glance, and went on —

"Fer a time the four on 'em will hang about this plantation — but only fer a time."

He paused as though he were searching for a word, and then, having found it, he proceeded —

"Then there will come upon the two little cocks the wanderin' fever. It's some German contraption," he added, apologetically.

"I know what you mean," I said. "You mean the 'roving impulse,' — the 'wanderlust.'"

"Aye, that's it," he said. "Well, that rovin' impulse 'll drive 'em far afield — it turns 'em into little adventurers. But the hen birds are stay-at-homes and will live about their native coverts."

"And other young cock-birds will, in search of adventure, come to this district and fill their places?" I said.

"That's right," he replied, "and that's how Natur' preserves the race. Humans must 'ave their laws, but the Wild has its instinct."

★   ★   ★

As I went home that day, I looked at the birds with new eyes. Everywhere there was vibrant health, alertness, *joie-de-vivre*. Each one seemed to chirp "I have the secret."

I wondered whether it would not be worth while for us humans to ponder more on some of the secrets of their well-being.

We seek diligently after health. They live naturally and health finds them. Perhaps it is a much surer way.

CHAPTER
FIVE

The Art of Making Butter

FEBRUARY

I live in a city. My work is there, and I love it. Were it not for the rush and excitement of town life, I hardly think I should appreciate the countryside as I do. City life acts as a foil to what I find in the fields.

When I set my face towards the open country, I leave speed and rush far behind, and find myself in a world where time-limits are not supreme.

I felt this as Raq and I sat in the kitchen of the farm, though this, perchance, is the one place in the countryside where bustle still reigns. There is not much "holiday" for the women-folk on a farm. From early morn until the afternoon milking is over, they have little time to themselves. Hannah and Charlotte are no exceptions to the rule. They have others to help them, it is true, but on a farm the mistress works as hard as the servant, and their hours are longer. Yet even in the kitchen there is no suggestion of frenzied haste. They work until their task is done; not as we in the city do, until the time of some evening entertainment or social duty calls us out.

"Tick — tock; Tick — tock," I hear the old grandfather clock say. Its beat is leisurely, measured. My clock at home ticks as though each second were trying to overtake time itself. When it strikes the hour it does so suddenly, stabbing the quiet of the house with an alarm note and with the arrogance of a tyrant. But the farm clock says "Take — time; Take — time," and

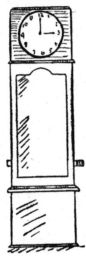

the pendulum seems to linger at the apex of each swing. Even when it strikes the hours, it gives warning. There is a whirring of inner machinery as though the wheels inside were awakening from a nap — as though they had to be reminded that they were needed at least once in the hour.

Through the window I see also the tonic of timelessness. The horses are walking up the track that leads to the High Barn. Bob, Alan's man, is by their side. Now and then they stop to sniff at some herbage by the hedge-side, and Bob lights his pipe. A word, and they are off again until they come to a closed gate, where they stand patiently until it slowly swings back. Their work lies over the brow of the hill — they will get there — some time. "Clip — clop; Clippety-clop," I can hear their hoofs striking against the rocky surface of the road. The sound has the same unhurried beat which marks the old clock.

★   ★   ★

There is a door at the far end of the farm kitchen. This leads into a kind of small larder. Then a few steps descend into the stone-flagged dairy, with its broad slate shelves.

Here stands the churn, and as I sat by the fire I could see Charlotte grasping its handle, and hear the rhythmic thud of its contents.

As Alan and Joe were out, I went to have a look at Charlotte making her butter.

"Is it nearly ready?" I asked.

Charlotte shook her head. "It takes longer in cold weather," she answered with a smile, pausing from her work for a moment and pressing a knob on the top of the barrel.

"Sounds as though you've punctured the thing," I said, as I heard a fizzing noise coming from the knob.

"I'm only lettin' the gas out," she answered, giving the screws which fasten on the lid an extra twist or two.

"What temperature ought the cream to be when you start churning?" I asked.

THE ART OF MAKING BUTTER

"Oh, about 56 to 60 degrees," she answered. "O' course, in summer the difficulty is to keep it cool. There's allus something to contend with. In winter it's slow work because the cream is cold. But the great thing in churning is to get your cream well mixed afore you start — then it's fairly plain sailing."

"I'll take the handle for a minute or two if you like," I said. I stressed "minute or two," for I have learned a few things in my time. First of all, that which to a townsman looks so easy often proves exhausting in a few moments. Also, if you take over any job from Charlotte, she doesn't stand by idly watching — she herself starts some other work, and you are left to finish what you have begun.

This is what actually did happen in spite of my hinting at a time-limit.

I found myself turning — turning — turning. The first few minutes were easy going. Then I found myself changing hands, for my right shoulder was feeling the strain. Then, when the left gave out, I went back to the right grip again. But the right soon got tired, so I took hold of the handle and churned with both hands, whilst all my underclothing gradually crept upwards until it ringed itself as a solid tourniquet round my neck.

I found my thoughts turning with sympathy to men who spend long hours gripping handles. "Pity the poor organ-blowers in our churches," I thought, and I made up my mind that I would in future choose more C.M.s (common metres) than 8.8.8.8.8.8. (six-eights). Then, too, I could have wept when I thought of thousands of wives who toil at the mangles on washing-day.

Then Hannah came to have a look at me. At first I thought I was to be reprieved, but I saw that her hands were covered with flour, and I groaned inwardly.

"How are you getting on?" she asked.

"Fine," I said gallantly, wiping my brow. "Is it nearly ready?"

"Charlotte'll be back in a minute," said she cheerily, and went back to her cooking.

I started to churn again. "In a minute," Hannah had said. I know those country "minutes." They are like country "miles," which are town miles multiplied by five. That is the worst of being in the country — time is

so slow! I found myself turning the churn to poetry. Lines of Tom Hood fitted in with its revolutions —

> Churn — churn — churn,
> While the cock is crowing aloof:
> And churn — churn — churn
> Till the stars shine through the roof!
> It's oh! to be a slave
> Along with the barbarous Turk,
> Where woman has never a soul to save
> If this is Christian work!

I looked through the door. Glorious sound! I heard the voices of Alan and Joe, and Charlotte telling them I was in the dairy, churning. With a new spirit of energy I seized the handle —

Oh! men with sisters dear!
Oh! men with mothers and wives,
It's not your churn your wearing out,
But human creatures' lives.

In another minute I saw the smiling faces of the two brothers beaming at me through the door. The next moment the churn was idle, and we were shaking hands, and Joe was thumping me on the back with the heartiest of welcomes.

"Isn't it ready?" said I inquiringly.

Charlotte took the lid off, and I gazed in, expecting to see great pounds of butter floating in a sea of whey; but all I could see was a quantity of creamy liquid that had little sign of butter in it.

"It's not ready yet," and looking at me, she added, "I've known it take a'most half-a-day sometimes in winter."

As she said this I edged away from the handle, and I was relieved when I saw Joe take hold of it. With an ease which comes from practice, he turned it as though he could go on untiringly for a month.

"Haven't ye a drop o' 'newkled' i' the hoose?" asked Alan. "That ud hurry it up a bit, I reckon."

Charlotte shook her head, and I wondered what "newkled" was. I thought that it was some patent mixture which hurried on the process of butter-making.

I was on the point of asking what it was when Alan said, "'Newkled,' you know, is cream from a newly-calved coo. You just mix a little with the rest in the churn — and there ye are!"

Fearful lest I might be asked to start again, I slipped into the kitchen. From my comfortable corner I could see Joe turning the churn.

Later I heard Charlotte say that it was "broken." Then I heard the sound of running liquid, and knew that the whey was being run off.

Just before we sat down to dinner, Charlotte to my surprise scalded her hands, saying, "It keeps the butter from stickin' to them, you know."

"And what more have you to do?" I asked.

"Oh," she said, "not a great deal. Just work the water out on't, and work salt in't, and then knock it into shape with 'Scotch hands.'"

"And how much do you get a pound for it?" I asked.

"Oh! one-and-nine a pound," she replied. "How much do you pay for it in town?"

"I don't know," I answered; "that is my wife's department. The study has no dealings with the kitchen, you know."

"Ye'll give up to half-a-crown, I reckon," said Alan. "It's not the farmer who mak's the profit," he added, shaking his head ruefully.

Thinking of that terrible handle and my aching shoulders, I said, "I should want four-and-six a pound if I had the making of it."

Whereat they all laughed, and we gathered round the table.

★　★　★

"Ever hear the yarn of the old couple who lived here before my grandfather? — how he made butter?" asked Joe.

I shook my head.

"He was a very careful man," said Alan, with a sly wink at me and stressing "careful" a little.

"Well," said Joe, "the old woman used to put t' cream in the churn and leave it standin' all neet."

"Wi' the lid off," added Charlotte.

"Aye," said Joe; "wi' the lid off. Well, next mornin' she fixed the lid on, and the old man started to churn. He noticed that it didn't go round wi' its usual swing, and called oot, 'Mother, what's wrang wi' t' churn?'

"'Nowt's wrang so far as I know,' replied the old lady.

"But he still persisted that 'summat were up wi' it,' so she came and took the lid off, and they both looked in."

Joe paused for a moment, and Charlotte and Hannah looked gravely at me. Alan was gazing up at the ceiling and rubbing the back of his head.

"'What's that black thing floatin' round?' asked the old man, 'that's not butter.' The old lady stared into t' churn wi' eyes that stuck oot like organ-stops. 'Sakes alive!' said she, 'it's oor cat!'"

"Dead as a turnip," added Alan.

Joe nodded.

"Then as she took the drooned beast and were aboot to throw it away, the —"

"It had fell in during the night," said Hannah quietly.

"Aye," said Joe, "it had. Well, as she were aboot to throw it away, the old man called oot, 'Stripe her, mother, stripe her.'"

"Stripe her?" I questioned. Whereat every one had a good laugh.

"He meant," said Charlotte, "scrape all the cream off her, so as not to waste any."

"He were a very careful man," said Alan, giving me another wink.

CHAPTER
SIX

The Spectre of the Night

SEPTEMBER

John Rubb and I were having our last day's fishing of the season. Not that we were expecting to get a big basket, for the rivers were still without much fresh water. But there is joy in the music of the stream, and the trees, rich in browns, scarlets and purples, give the sense of quiet gladness. I had a feeling that my rod knew that it was soon to be stowed away, and its foreknowledge of impending inactivity took away something of its whippiness.

As we wended our way in the morning light down to the river, we passed a brook which ordinarily ripples in joyous song to join the river. Now it was but a tiny trickle, and must have been afraid that even a bird would drink it dry.

Along its banks stood old trees, their trunks sawn off about twelve feet from the ground. Above these, graceful long shoots sway in the autumn breeze.

"Pollard willows," said John, as I stopped to look in one whose trunk was hollow. "Any old owl or bats having a sleep there?"

I shook my head. "Nothing but a lot of what looks like moist brown peat dust, clinging to the inside."

Not being very far from our first stream, John sat down to put on his waders.

"There was a rare talk some years ago," said he, "of a ghost owl that was to be seen flittin' about these fields at night. Some o' the farmers told me that they had seen something flying about and it glowed like a fire. You should have heard some of the descriptions of it that I got from the cottagers — 'Eyes glowin' like storm-lamps, and wings afire — it looked like Satan let loose.'"

John had a quiet chuckle as he recalled the gossip which had been readily regaled to him and had lost nothing in the telling.

"Of course," he continued, "I thought some of 'em had seen it when they were coming home late from the inn. Men do see queer things, I'm told, on such occasions. But the women-folk were positive, and told how it had brushed against them in the dark and skeered 'em to death. Go over and have another look at that hollow trunk."

Again I almost squeezed myself inside the old willow, but I could find no clue that would have warranted me in even making a guess as to the cause of the ghost owl.

By this time we were both ready for the river, and, as we walked on, John continued, "I was coming home one night in July. I had been trying to get hold of a

sea-trout and it was gettin' on for midnight. Suddenly I heard the 'Hoo-Hoo-ter-Hoo-Hoo' of an owl. It quavered off into the silence o' the night, and the next minute I saw a shining thing come like a spectre over the willows. I must say that for a moment it gave me a queer feeling here" — and John pointed somewhere in the region of his third waistcoat button.

"The ghost owl?" I murmured. "It was a reality, then, right enough?"

John nodded. "It came so sudden like that I involuntarily ducked, and as I did so, my eye caught something glowing in that old willow. What do you think I found when I went and examined it?"

"Glow worms," I said, hazarding a guess.

He shook his head. "A blue light shimmerin' on that moist peaty dust you found in there — it was all aglow with some kind o' phosphorescence."

"Something like the shimmer one sees on fish as it lies in the larder?" I asked.

"Just like that," John answered. "You see it sometimes on a fine summer night by the sea — every wave as it trips on to the shore is rimmed with shinin' blue. Myriads o' little infusoriæ, lit up like fairy-lamps, are the cause of it."

For the moment my mind wandered to those beautiful shores by which I have sat and watched those fairy waves. I could see the dark stretch of many waters before me, with the sea so calm that the stars used it as a mirror. Then would come the quiet swish of the wavelet as it broke upon the beach, and at the edge of the turmoil, the fringe of blue fire.

I was recalled from my reverie by hearing John say, "And then I knew the secret of the ghost owl."

I looked at him, not being able for the moment to link up the old willow tree with the appearance of the bogey of the night, so my friend continued —

"I should think that that brown dust must have been alive with little glowin' things, such as you've seen in the waves, and the old owl must have used the willow as his roosting-place, and —"

"And he got so well dusted with the 'light' powder," I broke in, "that when he issued forth into the night, he looked like an illuminated Christmas card."

"That's the secret of the ghost owl right enough," said John, giving his rod a preparatory flick or two.

★　★　★

As we entered the water I looked at my watch. It was half-past ten, and Raq, as he saw the stream in front of me, took up his usual position on the bank, awaiting with interest my need of the landingnet if good luck attended my efforts.

The opposite bank was lined with hazel bushes, and I could see the full nuts bearing down the slender branches. A rustle in the leaves attracted my attention, and for a moment I saw the dainty dancing figure of a dormouse. He had been visiting his larder, and was making the most of it ere the lean time begins, when he tucks his tail carefully over his sensitive nose, sleeping to the lullaby of the strong winds.

On the bank, a few rabbits dozed in the autumn sunshine. Raq saw them too, and looked at me with pleading in his eyes — pleading that he might be allowed to swim the river and scatter the drowsy family. This, however, would have spoiled my chances of getting a trout, and I shook my head at him.

How saucy rabbits are when they know a stream lies between them and a probable enemy! Hardly one moved as I advanced into the water, but I knew they were keeping a close scrutiny on my every movement.

For a moment or two I drank in the scene before me. In some of the fields boys and girls were out with baskets "brambling." I could hear their laughter above the lilt of the waters.

Far away toward the fells I could see the tiny white spots of sheep browsing on the heights. It will not be long now ere the shepherds will be bringing their charges towards the lowlands for the winter. When the sheep turn their heads towards the glades, then the trout begin to turn their heads upwards towards the little becks which have their rise in the hills. And, conversely, when the sheep once more move towards the heights in spring, the winter storms being a thing of the past, then the angler knows that the trout are once more down in the river, and his joys begin.

I was turning these things over in my mind when my line tightened. But I struck too late, and the fish got away. It was the only chance that I had that morning, and it caught me day-dreaming. It is always the unexpected that happens.

When John joined me later he had three fish to his credit — not bad fishing considering that it was late September and that the river was as clear as crystal — but then John is an angler, and compared with him, I am only a fisherman.

"What flies did you use?" I asked, as we sat down to enjoy a quiet smoke.

He held up to me some of his own favourites. He had no standard pattern, but all his lures were of the "shadow" type.

"What are their names?" I asked.

He shook his head. "I can't say. I'm no great believer in certain colours or certain shapes. When a trout wants his breakfast, I don't think he stops to look at complexions, or count whether an insect has six or sixteen legs. What I aim at is natural shape and size as near as I can make 'em, but keepin' 'em on the soft gauzy side."

"On the ghost owl plan — shadowy and spectral," I said, with a smile.

"Something like that," John answered, and though little luck was to be expected, down he went to the river again, with the hope that springs eternal in the angler's breast.

★ ★ ★

Later on, when dusk deepened into darkness, we met again, and for the sheer joy of the thing, kindled a fire and imbibed the smell of smoking pine-wood.

Nearly all wild things had gone to sleep. The sounds which still caught our ears were muffled. The hunters of the night were wide awake.

"And what's the catch?" I asked.

"A couple more," John said, "though this sea-trout hasn't seen the sea for many a day."

In the glow of the fire I could see that the silvery shine of the fresh run trout was absent. The scales were almost bronze, and the dark sheen of the back had lost its polish.

"If that fish were to stay in the river a few more months, it would return to the natural colour of the brown trout from which it sprung," said he. "How easily anything slips back to its natural state!" he added musingly. Then after a moment he sighed, "I lost a big one in the strong water over there."

"How big do you think it was?" I asked, lifting a warning finger. "Careful, now!"

John laughed. "I should think it would be over two pounds."

"Oh, moderate man!" said I. "I believe you are reforming."

As we trudged homewards I said, "Did you ever hear the story of the weighing of the baby?"

John shook his head.

"A new baby had come to a very remote cottage. It was the first, and the proud parents were anxious to know its weight, but had no means of gratifying their wish. They had no neighbours near, but by good luck, they remembered that a couple of anglers were in the neighbourhood, and some one in the house volunteered to find them and to borrow their angler's scales. When at last they arrived, the family gathered round with great expectation to see the 'weighing in' ceremony. The pointer of the spring balance stopped at twenty-five pounds!"

John stopped for a moment to light his pipe, and I could see his eyes twinkling in the flickering light.

"A well-nourished child," was all he said.

CHAPTER
SEVEN

Shearing Sheep

JUNE

For the first time for many weeks Raq and I walked on moist land. As the dog brushed through the long grass of the hedge-bottoms, so they sprayed him with shining drops. How green the leaves appeared! Trees and hedges had had their faces washed free from dust, and the herbage, weary with the drought, was looking young again.

Even the birds were beginning to sing. What a tragic time the nurseries have had! The relentless dryness had practically exterminated the insect life on which the parent birds depended for the youngsters' diet, and one by one a brood of four had dwindled to an emaciated one. Even the survivor, though he had managed to find his wings, yet found the earth too hard to probe with his amateurish diggings.

Down in what once were marshes, the birds of the mire and swamp had found only hard-baked, cracked mud. Plovers, snipe, and their kin must have been bereaved of their fluffy mites, looking in vain for the rain that meant salvation. In the rivers, too, the mortality amongst the fish has been great.

Now, however, the dog and I noticed that the birds had plucked up courage again. Even the thrush and blackbird, who usually store away their flutes when July approaches, were piping in the elms. The robin seemed to have lost some of his plaintiveness, and the wren sang a song which, for volume, made one think he must be the size of a stormcock.

As we neared the farm, we heard a big chorus of protesting, querulous bleatings. Scores of quavering questions fell from the throats of the lambs.

We were early enough to catch Alan and Joe going in to breakfast. This meal, as every one knows, is the one which prepares the way for the later "ten-o'clock." Neither I nor the dog were loath to follow them into the kitchen, where Hannah and Charlotte were busy with something which produced most appetizing odours.

"And what's the row going on amongst the sheep?" I asked, as we sat down to table.

"Joe's bin roundin' 'em up," answered Alan. "We're goin' to do a bit o' clippin' —"

"Shinglin'," Joe interpolated with a wink. "We must keep up wi' the times."

"Shearin'," corrected his brother with a smile, and then Hannah brought in the bacon and conversation stopped for a few minutes.

"I don't know how you manage it," I said, "but the flavour of your rashers is always the same. We get stuff in the town which tastes like fried tape. Yours, too, swims in most succulent 'dip.' Our town variety dries up like oak chips."

"What goes into the pig comes oot in the bacon," said Alan. "Good feedin' brings its dividend o' good flavour."

"And good curin'," added Joe, looking at his sisters.

"Brown sugar, salt, and saltpetre," said Charlotte, "well rubbed in, and then swung up near the rafters there, to mellow and ripen — that's the secret."

"And your lungs full o' fresh morning air making you ready for't," said Hannah; which was quite a long speech for her to make.

★　★　★

After our morning "crack" we made our way to the barn. I love this old building. From it stone steps creep up to the granary, where the robins always find ingress, and the spiders drape the rafters with mighty webs. In one corner of the barn stands the turnip cutter. To hear the sharp knives slicing their way through the turnips is a most appetizing sound.

The barn, still waiting for its loads of the new hay, had been cleared of all impediments. One end had a few hurdles placed across it — this made a pen for the "rough" sheep that had to be sheared. Outside, in the yard, the lambs bleated for the mothers who were waiting to be shorn of their locks. There were three "clippers" — Alan, Joe, and Bob, their man, who has been on the farm goodness knows how long. John, the farm pupil, stood ready to catch the ewes and take

them to Alan or Joe, and another lad stood ready to wrap up the fleece and carry it away to the granary.

As I watched John take hold of a full-grown sheep and dexterously fling it on its back, it looked such an easy operation that I thought I should like to have a try.

The sheep stood watching me through the pen. What curious eyes they have! They look at you without any emotion showing in their liquid pale grey orbs — only vacant fear lurks in them.

I laid hold of a good hefty ewe, and by the swift way its legs moved came to the conclusion that I had got hold of a centipede by mistake.

My left arm went under its throat, and my right stole over its back even as I had watched the "catcher" do it. I then gave it a mighty heave. But though I lifted the sheep, it came down on all fours, much to the delight of the shearers.

I tried again, and as the ewe felt the strain, she merely sat on her haunches, and her hind quarters appeared to weigh about three tons!

When the laughter had ceased, Alan called out —

"Start again, and when you've got owd on 'er, and you want to throw her on 'er back, press yer right knee well under her shoulder — you forgot the knee trick."

54

"A good 'old on her back, and a good shove wi' the knee, gives her a bit o' a spin — and ower she comes," supplemented Joe.

After such advice I found no difficulty in putting my sheep on her back.

"He'll mak' a farmer yet, I reckon," said Bob approvingly; so I felt I had acquitted myself fairly well.

★ ★ ★

Now the "clipper" is holding the overturned ewe between his knees. The sharp shears first of all open out the breast, and then lay bare the neck until they reach the shoulder. How pinky white the newly-exposed parts are!

I rubbed my hand over them, and no longer wondered how the wool turns the rain, for my hand was lubricated with the finest oil-cream.

"That's the best lanoline," said Joe.

"No better mackintosh in the world," added Alan.

The shears have now left the shoulder, and are working on that under-rotundity which is not mentioned in polite society. Then, after laying the beast on its right and left sides, the clippers finish their work over the backbone, and the much shrunken sheep stands once more upon its wooden-like legs, its head looking ridiculously large for the size of its body.

One of the lads approached the much-lightened animal, and before it left the barn, stamped on its left side in tar, a big letter P.

"That's to let every one know that a parson has had a hand i' fleecing the flock," said Joe, with a grin.

As I threatened him with bodily violence, he threw up his arms and cried, "Camerade," and Alan explained —

"Now that the sheep is so much slimmer, it can get through any small gap i' the hedge, so we brands 'em well wi' oor own name. They are apt to stray on to a neighbour's land, you know," he added.

"What happens then?" I asked. "Have you to pay for their pasturage?"

Alan shook his head. "'Give and take' is the motter o' farmers, and we have grand neighbours."

"A feller called oot to me yesterday," said Joe, "'If you've lost a couple o' ewes, they are i' my field. But you needn't worry — they 'ave their teeth wi' 'em.'"

★　★　★

And so the work goes on. Every ten minutes a ewe is relieved of its wool, and about a hundred sheep are disposed of in the course of a day. What an illustration of the sunny side of socialism! Watch the relationship between masters and men on the farm which I call "mine." Alan and Joe are the masters, and the workers are their servants — but all have their heart in their work, and there is the lubrication of personal liking for each other.

"Aboot eight pounds o' wool comes off each sheep," says Alan, as the boy picks up the fleece.

"I've heerd it said," Joe says, as he tackles another ewe, "that a few years back, it took four sheep to dress a woman in clothes fer the year, but now —"

"I reckon it tak's aboot four silkworms," Alan said, with a laugh, and even the sheep appeared to enjoy the joke.

"Those waiting lambs are kicking up a din," I remarked. "They are evidently getting tired of waiting for their mothers."

"They'll get a shock, too, when they see 'em come oot shingled," said Alan.

"Some on 'em," Joe explained, "'ll have nowt to do wi' their mothers after we've finished wi' 'em.

"They look so strange to 'em, that it mak's 'em wean theirsels. It knocks 'em all of a heap to see their dams come to us like middle-aged matrons, and then skip oot like fifteen-year-old lasses."

★ ★ ★

As Raq and I went homeward we heard on a neighbouring farm the rattle of the cutter as it laid low the grass.

"Light crops there'll be this year, old man," I said to the dog, as I looked at the long lanes of the newlymown.

Raq was lifting his nose to the gentle breeze that wafted over the fields. I, too, was drinking in the delicate flavours that it carried. But the dog was hoping to catch some scent of game; he knew nothing of the clover fragrance, or of the spicy aroma exuding from the juicy stems of the slain grasses.

Then, as the cutter ceased for a moment, I heard the call of a cock partridge. For weeks that field had been the home of his mate and her little family. Now the sanctuary was laid bare, and the field looked strange and unfamiliar.

"He's protesting against the shearing of his protecting green," I said to the dog. "Lucky for him and his family that the young corn still stands as a refuge!"

I stood still for a moment imbibing the sweet scent of the new-mown field. Then I turned to the dog and said —

"Many a thing is taken from us in this world, and we call it a loss. 'Weaning' may be a different term for it — the same thing looked at from a different angle."

"I agree, master," wagged Raq's tail, but his nose said, "Let me go after that old partridge."

CHAPTER
EIGHT

Gossamer

SEPTEMBER

Raq and I were in our quiet village again. What a flavour it has, especially after existing in the city. Its lichened walls, its thatched roofs, the sound of the lowing of kine, the squeal of young pigs and the rumble of a farmer's cart over cobbled ways, seem to retain the past and make it vibrant in the present.

As we walked down its main street, where friendly and inquisitive faces peeped at us from behind white curtains and pots of geraniums — drawing back into the shadow as we drew nearer — Sally Stordy came to her door and greeted me with —

"Come in a minute; I've got a bit o' yer faverite."

I entered her bright kitchen and Sally from her store produced a blackberry-and-apple plate-cake.

"Lucky ye 'appened to come to-day. Childer has got 'em from the woods," she said, pointing to the juicy berries that peeped through a hole in the centre. "It ud all a bin gone by neet."

I must say that I enjoy Sally's plate-cakes — "tarts" they call them in certain districts, and Sally knows how to make them — fruit and pastry travel together right to the edge.

"Oor Jim finishes schoolin' next month," said she, taking off her apron in honour of my visit.

"And what are you going to make him?" I asked, thinking of the lad with his shock of red hair and healthy, freckled face.

"That's where we're beat," admitted his mother. "Sometimes I reckon he'd mak' a butcher — he's bin a killer since he were a little 'un; never 'appier than when he's swattin' flies or cuttin' up worms or buryin' summat as 'e's killed like."

"What about an undertaker?" I said gravely.

Sally shook her head. "There's only a hundred on us in t' village, and if he buried every one of us there'd 'ardly be a livin' in it. O' course," she added, "he could do odd jobs while he were waitin' in-be-times."

She paused a moment to cut me another liberal slice, and added — "His father thinks as 'ow he might do well in a bank, fer he can keep any money he gets better'n all the rest o' th' family, and mak' it go farther an' all. I've heerd his father say of him, 'He can spread a small bit o' butter on a bigger piece o' bread better'n any on us.' See, how many have you?"

"Two," I answered, "boy and girl."

"An' I've seven," she said thoughtfully, and I could see she was thinking of the future, and wondering, mother-like, how they were to be settled in the world.

60

* * *

The dog and I turned from the village and cut through the fields. Every view was veiled in white mist, through which the sun was beginning to make its presence felt. The whole countryside no longer hummed with feverish activity, but seemed to be enjoying quiet evening hours. Every hedge purred with the joy of achievement — the promise of the Spring, spelt in bridal blossoms, now fulfilled itself in fruit. Hips and haws swung scarlet amidst tired leaves. Ebony blackberries and acorns invited all to come to a feast. For this season — plants and grasses had lived — the continuity of the race was assured.

From the hedge the spaniel flushed a couple of cock pheasants, resplendent in bronze, blue and crimson. What a rush and a scurry they made as they leapt high in the air, and, with deceptive flight, sped towards a neighbouring wood! Raq watched them with a reproachful glance, as though he thought they were taking an unfair advantage by leaving him on the ground.

"Only a few more days, old man," I said, referring to the birds, "and their days of peace will be over. October

will soon be here, and then —" I put my arms up as I would do were I handling a gun, and Raq looked expectantly ahead.

Seeing it was only make-believe he trotted on to search for more trails — probably for him also the joy was in the tracking more than in the finding.

Walking across a distant field we spied the figure of Ned, for whom we were looking, and the old postman signalled to us to accompany him on his rounds.

For a time I gave him a full account of my recent wanderings. Then, as I rambled on, the stillness was broken by the shouts of young life which reached us from the distant village school.

"Play-time," said Ned laconically.

With Sally Stordy's conversation in my mind, I said musingly —

"I wonder whether those youngsters will become farmers."

"It's hard to say," said Ned slowly. "One or two on 'em will take up farmin', but most on 'em, if I'm any judge, 'll want what I call 'kid-glove' occupations."

He looked hard at me to see if I understood what he meant, and seeing my nod he continued —

"What they'll be I can't say, but I'll bet that there'll be no plumbers or bricklayers among 'em, and few joiners either. Most on 'em 'll want to be clerks and teachers and such like. It seems to me that in a few years' time the old sort o' craftsmen 'll be non — non —"

"Non-existent," I hinted.

"Aye," he said slowly, but disappointedly. "I was thinkin', though, of a forrin word that ye once used."

"*Non est?*" I said.

His eyes lighted up at that, and he pronounced the forgotten phrase with evident relish.

★ ★ ★

As we crossed over a field I stooped to refasten my shoe-lace, and as I did so called Ned's attention to the glittering surface of the ground.

My companion knelt down for a moment, used his bent fingers as a miniature rake, and there glistened on them scores of fine silken threads.

"Cobwebs," I said.

"Gossamer," he corrected, and in such a tone that I knew he had found a subject on which he could expound.

"And behind each thread," said Ned, disentangling one from the mass and holding it up with the dark hedge as a background, "lies adventure and romance. Know anything aboot spiders?"

"Only that I shouldn't care to be Mr. Spider," I said.

"Ah," he said slowly, "then you've heerd that the missus would just as soon eat her man as she would a fly?"

"It's a kind of affection that is a trifle too absorbing for my liking," I answered.

"There's two sides to every story," Ned answered, "but I'll stick to gossamer fer a minute or two."

I signified assent by finding a convenient seat, and still holding up the thread and keeping his eyes fixed on it as though he were seeking inspiration the old postman began —

"Spiders 'ave their problems with their families just as we 'ave. They have so many childer that they 'ardly know what to do wi' 'em. Some on 'em carry their families aboot tucked away on their bodies."

"Something like the mothers who carry their babies on their backs swathed in a shawl," I interpolated.

"Same idee," said Ned; "only roond the spider there are hundreds on 'em."

"She must be nearly tickled to death," I said, imagining the effect of scores of wriggling bodies on the parent stem.

"Howsomever," said Ned, ignoring my last remark, "the time comes when the food problem must be faced. Winter lies ahead with its scarcity, and the adult spider will have all her work cut oot to satisfy her own hunger, let alone to fill the mouths of her young 'uns."

Ned looked at me to see whether I was getting the "hang" of his explanation, so I said —

"The problem for the spider is, then, 'How can I "place" my children in the big world?' There may be enough food in their own homeland for a few, but not for thousands."

"Ye've got it," said my companion, "and the youngsters solve the problem fer themselves by becomin'" — here he braced himself before delivering his next few words — "colonists, parachutists, aeronauts."

★   ★   ★

As he looked as though he expected me to applaud, I turned to Raq, who was gravely looking on, and said —

"Hold on a minute. You've nearly choked my dog with that last mouthful. Do you know, old man," I said, addressing Raq, "what a parachutist or aeronaut is?" The dog in answer simply sidled up to me and lifted his head for a caress. "It's one who does not know whether he'll stay in the aer-or-naut, see?"

Ned smiled, though I half-expected he would snort with impatience. I suppose he was really pleased that I had taken notice of his big words.

Ned continued —

"One mornin' in Autumn when the air is still, save fer the warm currents risin' from the ground, and ripples o' breezes that Natur' puffs o'er the fields now and then, these youngsters decide that the time 'as come fer 'em to make a move."

"To emigrate," I said.

"Ye can watch 'em crawl up some post or bush where the wind can sweep. They get up to the highest point, and turnin' their heads towards the comin' breeze, raise their tails in the air."

The story-teller paused for a moment whilst a neighbouring robin set his words to plaintive sweet music.

"Then, three or four strands o' finest silk appear on the end of their tails — it's a liquid that comes oot o' their bodies and sets hard-like as soon as the air breathes on it. The strands join up and form one thread, and as the wind comes along the youngster pays out her line, fine as a silken thought."

The robin sang on, and it seemed to me that he had entered into the spirit of Ned's story, and, like a good orchestra, was working up his theme to a dramatic finish.

"Now, as the breeze grows stronger," continued Ned, and I could see he had forgotten my presence and with his inner eye was seeing what he described, "so the silken threads float out, and as they flap in the wind the 'pull' on the little adventurer grows stronger. Now and then he is a'most lifted off his legs. Soon he has enough sail oot — a puff o' wind catches his pen — pen —"

"Pennon," I said quietly.

"Pennon," continued Ned, "and some inner voice calling, 'Let go,' away he floats, to descend at nightfall, perchance, in an unknown country, there to make a new home and to make his way in the world — an emigrant and colonizer."

"Can he descend when he wants to?" I asked, fascinated with the picture of that living kite.

Ned nodded. "All he has to do is to coil in his line."

"And to set more sail if he wants to go further, I suppose?" I asked.

"That's aboot it," said Ned. "And when he alights, he leaves his sail behind him. Some call it cobwebs — that's prose. But those who are in the know call it 'Gossamer' — and that's poetry."

He picked up a thread discarded by some little voyager.

"Can ye see its rainbow tints?" he asked reverently.

And when I nodded my head in assent he said —

"The tints are woven into the name — Gossamer."

"It's a compound of sheen and shimmer," I concluded, and by the way the old man took my arm I knew he enjoyed the conceit.

CHAPTER
NINE

The Feather Seekers

JANUARY

"Well," said I to John Fell, as Raq and I joined him outside his cottage, "anything fresh?"

"The year has turned," he said thankfully; "that's the best bit o' news fer anybody, I reckon."

"Just by a few moments — a little longer dusk — the door of day swinging back an inch or two wider," I said.

John nodded. "But there are other signs, ye know, which are just as sure as the lengthening days."

I waited for him to continue.

"If ye'll look carefully, ye'll notice a little spirit o' gallantry creepin' into some o' the ways o' the birds, and also ye'll see that already the blue feathers o' the tits are lookin' as though they've bin dry-cleaned, and the cock is willin' to tolerate the presence o' the hen when there's food about."

"Isn't he always glad to see her then?" I asked.

"Every man fer hisself is the law o' the fields when winter mak's things scarce. Consequently, if Mr. Cock finds a tit-bit, and a little hen-bird appears, then he's as savage wi' her as he is wi' a rival. But now he's willin' to offer her a seat i' the 'bus, so to speak, and thinks o' takin' off 'is hat to her, instead o' peckin' her, when she hops along."

"That reminds me of something I've been wanting to ask you for some time," I said.

John looked at me expectantly, but said nothing.

"You know those long-tailed tits," I began, "those —"

"Those I pointed out to ye in the pine-wood yonder?" asked he.

I nodded and continued —

"Well, why have they such long tails, while the little blue tits have tiny things that appear to be as much use to them as the wren's?"

John shook his head and said —

"Now you've asked me something. If I tell ye that they act as balancin' poles, ye will say that there's no better acrobats than the short-tailed blue 'uns. And what's more, they aren't such good hunters o' the bark and crevices as 'Bluey.' Can't think why their tails are so long." He thought for a moment, and then said: "Now it's my turn to ask ye summat. 'Have ye ever thought what she does wi' her tail when she's sitting on 'er eggs? Ye remember the nest I showed ye?'"

"Domed one, thick felt-like moss, feather-lined, and in shape like a Jenny Wren's," I answered readily.

"Good," said my companion approvingly; "but what becomes of her long tail when she enters that little cave? Ye never see it become real ragged or slattern-like."

"She might push it through the felt dome," I hazarded.

"And so let oot all the heat i' the nest, and cause a cold draught to blow on t' eggs," said John, a trifle sarcastically. "Nay, lad, that won't do. Just think fer a minute, and ye'll notice that nearly all the birds which mak' a nest wi' a lid on have stumpy tails — kingfisher —"

"In a hole," I said.

"Dipper and wren," continued John; and I nodded to show that I saw he had mentioned these in order to emphasize the unusualness of a bird with a long tail building an enclosed home.

"Well," said he, "she goes in, settles on her eggs, and then curls her tail over her back and head, and ye can see the tips o' the tail feathers peepin' through the entrance. I don't think I know a neater way o' gettin' rid of a hindrance than that."

★ ★ ★

John wanted to visit some of his rabbit traps, so the dog and I took the chance of accompanying him.

As we went along, the keeper said suddenly —

"Afore we get to 'The Ridge' covert, just try and see how many feathers ye can count lyin' aboot i' the fields, hedge-bottoms, or anywhere."

I looked at him curiously to see whether he was playing a joke on me, but I saw by his expression that he was serious.

70

"I'd bet a dollar that ye don't get a hundred," said he, and then relapsed into silence.

Going through the first field I felt that my task would be an easy one. I found twenty-five, most of them coming from the poultry which John kept.

Then, as we left the cottage further behind, I had difficulty in finding any. Look where I would, everything came to light except a feather. Even through one of the woods I only found two, and these had fallen from the rump of a wood-pigeon.

"Well," said John, when we reached his traps, "how many?"

"Thirty-seven," I said, with a rather crestfallen air, but still curious as to John's reason for setting me the task.

The keeper was on the point of saying something, but checked himself. "Then," said he, as though speaking to himself, "I wonder whether that long-tailed tit's nest is still here," and without another word he strode away through the wood, leaving Raq and me by the small stile that led into the covert.

I knew where he was making for — a thick bush behind his hut, where deftly woven materials of moss, lichen, cobwebs and feathers might possibly be still intact.

In a few moments I heard John returning, and he handed to me a portion of the long-tailed tit's former home.

"There's only aboot a quarter left; but I should like ye to count the feathers whilst I go around to my traps. It's no place for Raq; he might get his legs i' their jaws."

I pulled the nest to pieces, and by the time the keeper returned I still had not finished my counting.

"How many?" asked John.

"So far, four hundred and forty-eight," I answered.

"That'll do then," said John. "Ye see that in that nest there'll a bin aboot two thousand on 'em, when it were fresh-built."

He paused and waited to see whether I had now caught the drift of his remarks, and why he had asked me to see how many feathers I could find in the fields and in the woods.

"And I did not find fifty in a stretch of a mile and a half," I said.

"That's the point," said John, shaking his head appreciatively; "and how do them tiny little mites find two thousand on 'em lyin' aboot?"

"They may find a dead bird and use up its feathers," I hazarded.

"Aye, they might," answered the keeper, "but they're not the only ones on the look oot fer beddin' — there's willow-wrens and other tits, redstarts, wrens, wagtails, linnets, and sparrers. All of 'em use feathers, and it seems to me the demand must be pretty large, and the supply 'pears to be rather scanty."

As we were returning, John said —

72

"Just think o' the miles them little tits must travel in findin' and then carrying them two thousand feathers back to the site. But o' course they'll need 'em."

I looked at him as he made the last remark. Why should the little tit need them more than the thrush or the blackbird? I asked myself mentally.

When John noticed that I made no remark, he must have guessed what I was thinking, for he said —

"Ye see, such a tiny speck o' life won't have too much heat to give away from that little body o' 'ers, and she'll have anything from eight to a dozen eggs to cover, sometimes more. Which 'ud you rather sleep on — a hair mattress or a feather bed?"

"For warmth," said I, throwing to the winds all my principles of hygiene, "give me the feather bed."

"That's why, I reckon, the long-tailed tit gathers so many feathers, and hygiene or no hygiene, every one o' them tiny specks o' life seems to come oot 'ale and hearty."

★ ★ ★

As we passed through one of the woods, Raq, with evident delight, flushed a cock pheasant. Right up from a low-lying bush it went, and, with whirring wings, flashed through an opening left by the tall branches of the pine trees — a streak of bronze and purple shooting up into a tiny patch of blue sky.

"There's another fellow wi' a long tail," commented my companion. "Ever examined it?"

"I've noticed," I said, "that its tail has black diagonal lines on it."

"That's to tally wi' the stems o' reeds and bushes, so that it can hardly be seen when standin' or lyin' among 'em. But why are the feathers so long?" he asked.

I did not answer at once, so my friend asked another question —

"Which can ye steer wi' best, a long oar or a short un?"

"No need to answer that," I said.

"Well," said the keeper, "why has the partridge a short stumpy bunch of a tail?"

"You are always asking questions," I said, turning smilingly towards him.

"It's the only way to larn," he remarked simply, and, answering his own queries, continued —

"That there pheasant lives i' the woods. Sometimes, if an enemy comes along, his only way o' escape lies by shootin' up straight, and flying oot through the tiny patch o' clear space left by two or three trees. Consequently, he's got to have a good rudder trailin' behind so that he can hit that space clean and true. And the partridge?" he asked, looking directly at me.

"The partridge," I answered, "is a bird of the open fields, and only has straight hedges to negotiate, and the whole sky is open to him."

"True," said John; "there's a reason at the back o' all Nature's designs. There's no such thing as chance."

★ ★ ★

After John had left us I kept in my mind the question of how the long-tailed tit found her feathers.

By the side of the wood I found the dog standing by a stone and sniffing at the remnants of some small bird. It looked as though someone had stood on the stone and then plucked the bird, dealing out the feathers as though they were a pack of cards.

Raq looked up at me expectantly.

"Sparrow-hawk," said I, and as we looked at all that was left of a chaffinch, I heard the tits twittering in the pines. Raq, I thought, did not like the scent

which clung to the stone.

A little later we watched the flashing "stoop" of a peregrine-falcon. I am not quite sure what bird its victim was, but we saw it stagger and fall as the talons crashed into its back.

In the quiet afternoon air we saw the feathers descending. Just a few floated down like a wisp of smoke and then separated, sailing lightly down, down, down, as though carrying part of the brave spirit whose body had crashed to earth. Other birds might look on and with a shudder, shriek "Murderer" at the slate-blue phantom of death which had delivered the blow. But as I listened to the tits in the woods I fancied that, looking forward to the Spring, they remarked one to the other, "Those hawks may eat us — but they do provide good feather beds for us." And they went on with their twittering.

CHAPTER
TEN

Nature's Spring Cleaning

MARCH

As the dog and I left the main highway and turned up an enticing winding road, I said to him, "Raq, my boy, we leave the chara-ridden road and seek the haunts of ancient peace."

Whenever I speak with measured grandiloquence, the dog always realizes that I am in tip-top humour and shows his appreciation by rubbing himself affectionately against my leggings.

"In other words," I said, "we are making for Sally Stordy's."

He signalized my return to common speech by rolling over on his back, and then by racing round in circles. As a matter of fact, the day was so beautiful and the air so fresh, that I would like to have run riot also.

But when we reached the village, I noticed that the windows wore an unwonted appearance. Gone were the white curtains, so easy to look through from behind.

Gone also were the small tables on which rested the aspidistra, or the geraniums which never seemed to tire of blooming.

Some of the windows were quite unashamedly naked, others had sheets of newspaper pinned across. Behind the small panes also I noticed a pair of steps. Now I have a particular hatred of steps, as they have always to be put away after they have been used. A hammer or a pair of pliers can be laid down anywhere — left to the tidier.

Then, instead of the usual cackling of hens, the occasional grunt of an exploring sow, or the baritone resonance of calves waiting to be fed, I heard the sound of rhythmic beats. It was the death-knell of all my hopes. Someone was beating a carpet.

When I looked in at Sally's, my worst fears were confirmed. Everything seemed to be upside down. But she gave me her usual smile from underneath a close-fitting mob-cap.

"You are far too busy to bother with visitors," I said apologetically as I saw her armed cap-à-pie for the general mêlée of spring-cleaning.

"Come in," she said, beginning to undo her apronstrings.

This I have noticed is a characteristic action, almost a reflex action, of all women. Whether you find them at the wash-tub or busy baking, the first thing they do as they welcome you, is to slide their fingers to the knots, and cast the wretched sign of unpreparedness for visitors on one side. Often the apron is far cleaner than

78

what it hides, but it has the suggestion of the menial about it — so it must go.

"Well, you have caught me this time and no mistake," said she, taking a quick glance at herself in the mirror.

"We'll only stay a minute," I said, as I seated myself on a stool, Raq looking in vain for his customary mat.

"It'll do me no 'arm to sit a bit," said Sally. "I've bin at it sin' nigh six this mornin', and a cup o' tea'll set us both up, I reckon."

Protests were useless, and so, as she cleared a corner of the table, I said, "There seems to be a regular epidemic of cleaning going on."

"Aye," said she, "an' it'll mak' against t' meetin' in t' Chapil to-night, that it will. We're all a-cleanin' down fer Easter."

As Sally uttered the last words, I wondered why the phrase "cleaning up" refers to ordinary housework, whilst "cleaning down" is always reserved for the Spring campaign.

"Aye," she continued, "Ben Braisby's missus may be there — she's finished, or says she has. But she only had her curtins down a week, so she can't have bottomed it."

I can never hope to give Sally's expression of that curious word. Behind it lay all the frenzy of the fanatic, all the passion of a devotee, all the scorn she had for what she called "swish and flick cleanin'."

"None on us," she went on, "'as seen her 'room' carpet on t' grass either, so there must a bin some slithery work somewhere. Howsomever, she warn't brought up i' this district."

As she sipped her tea her indignation faded.

"There's Emma, now, bin helpin' t' vicar's wife. She sends her carpets to the laundry. But I don't hold wi' them methods. 'Do 'em yerself,' I say, 'and then ye know they're done.'"

"What about vacuum-cleaners?" I asked hopefully, remembering that I, too, had a home and a wife who was singularly liable to a similar attack.

"They're machinery," said Sally, "and there's nowt like a bit o' elbow grease."

She rose and went to the back door for a moment.

"My word," she said, with such undisguised admiration in her voice that I rose and followed her. "Susie Young is at it, I reckon." Through the orchard I could see a hedge covered with snow-white washing. "She's got 'em a good colour too — sheets, curtins, blankets (they look a bit thin), quilts . . ." Sally ticked them all off. "She'll be doin' 'er valances and 'er crewel-work mantel-border next. So she'll not be at t' Chapil neither."

The dog and I moved on.

How these village folks, I thought, like to have a reputation for cleanliness. That was the driving force behind all the pother in the little houses. Some people are proud of their wealth; others of their good looks. Those in the village like to be thought "clean." Many of them would have had the whole wretched upset finished in a week but for that reputation which was dear to them. Personally I should plump for a little less reputation and a little more speed. But I am a mere man.

★   ★   ★

Through the fields which led to the farm we wandered, and in one of them met Ned, with his bag of letters.

"The world's a fresh place this mornin'," was his greeting, and, as he lifted up his face towards the breeze, he asked, "Can't ye smell the spice in it and a'most hear the new life that's swellin' towards the sun?"

As we passed one of the woods, the pine trees swayed under the wind's gentle breath and wafted us of their best. We caught sight of the honeysuckle in tender green leaf, whilst the larch was preparing to show us her trailing glory.

"Sweet and clean," said Ned; "them's the words fer a mornin' like this."

The phrase was strangely reminiscent of one used by Sally Stordy, and I spoke to him of the frenzied revolution going on in the village.

"Well," said he, "Nature uses the same kind o' methods. There's a time fer peacefulness when the wind steals across yer face wi' a velvet touch, and when the

some of
NATURE'S SCAVENGERS

stream ambles along wi' a song in its heart. But when the gale is roarin' through the woods, uprootin' 'em and snappin' off the branches, and when the river thunders doon like a regiment o' cavalry — there ye have the power which prunes and cleans."

"And destroys," I added.

"Mebbe," said Ned; "but it seldom harms the strong — only the cracked and the weak. An' when the river settles doon agin, then the stones shine like jewels and every little creek has lost its rubbish. There's a time fer usin' the duster, and a time fer usin' the broom."

He was silent for a moment or two, and I knew that he was turning over the theme of our talk in his mind.

"Think on't," he said, "God A'mighty has more work to keep goin' than you think. Some people only imagine Him doin' the beautiful things i' life — makin' the grass grow and coaxing the colours to glow. But He often 'as a dirty world thrown on His hands. There's millions on us suckin' into oor lungs pure air, and by night I reckon we've blowed oot enough foul air to poison a continent. It's sweet agin by the mornin' becos He's got His filters to work."

The old man looked at me to see whether I was following him.

"Aye, filters," he repeated. "Don't ye know that the leaves drink in the poison that we breathe oot, sieve all the uncleanness oot on 't, and give us back the fragrance o' the mornin' as sweet as a bairn's breath. What does yer missus do wi' all the rubbish o' the hoose?"

"Puts it in the dust-bin," I said.

82

"And what do ye think becomes o' all the rubbish o' the countryside? Why is it that ye hardly ever see a dead bird or a decayin' mouse lyin' aboot? Think o' the dead fish i' the sea and rivers, the millions o' creepin' and crawlin' things that die daily. Why doesn't the world stink wi' rottenness and corruption?"

He paused and eyed me for a moment.

"Becos," he continued, "there's a sanitary department in the universe."

And with those words ringing in my ears he left me for a few moments to deliver his letters to a cluster of lime-washed cottages.

★   ★   ★

After leaving Ned a familiar figure came into view, and Raq bounded joyfully to greet Jerry.

I told him what we had been talking about, and he said, "The old man's right, ye know. I'll show ye summat if ye come along wi' me."

As we went over the fields Jerry paused at the base of an old hollow tree, and poking about amongst its roots, he brought to me half-a-dozen small rounded balls of a grey colour. In some of them were small skulls and bones. In others were traces of feathers.

"That's the castin's of an owl that's probably inside the holler there. Ye can see that it's made a meal o' mice and a bird or two. He swallers the lot and then throws up the indigestible bits — bones and feathers and sich like. That's why ye don't see too many dead 'uns lyin' aboot. Thousands on 'em don't have a chance to die

83

nat'rally. Natur' provides a live cemetery fer 'em. Owls and bats, weasels and hawks pick up the weak 'uns and the silly 'uns. Foxes and stoats keep swallerin' the surplus population. They are scavengers o' the weak 'uns, weeders oot o' the things which 'ud die and fester i' the sweet fields."

"We humans do just the opposite," I said. "Keep alive the weakling and —"

"Allow him to pass on his weakness to others," added Jerry, shaking his head ruefully.

Over by the hedge he paused and began to scratch out the sand which blocked a rabbit burrow. Soon there came to view the full-sized skeleton of a young rabbit. Every bone was as white as ivory.

"Nothin' disgustin' there," said my companion, pointing to the remains. "No decay, no taint or smell and the bones'll go to dust and fertilize the earth. Know what's bin at work?"

I shook my head.

"When bunny died," Jerry continued, "there were some keen noses not very far away, and some beetles aboot an inch long and with orange markin's came to the funeral."

"How many of them?" I asked.

"Pr'aps a dozen on 'em. They visited the scene o' the accident in couples — man and wife, ye know. Well," he continued, "it didn't suit their purpose to leave the body exposed. A hedgehog might find it and upset their funeral plans. So they set to work and dug a ditch all roond it."

"What did they dig with?" I asked, with growing interest.

"Strong jaws," answered Jerry, "so strong that the lot of 'em could have pulled the wee thing to a more suitable grave if they'd a wished. Then," he continued, "they dug another ditch inside the first one, fillin' up with the sand dug oot o' the second. They went on makin' these trenches till at last the little beggar were undermined, and then the weight o' his body sunk him lower and lower into his grave."

"Orange markings is not a very suitable colour for undertakers," I hazarded, just to brighten up the tale.

Jerry smiled and said, "Then, when it were deep

enough, the little female carrion beetles entered the dead rabbit, and laid their eggs, whilst the husbands did the navvyin' job o' coverin' it wi' sand."

"Real sextons," I said.

"At last they crept oot and went off to look fer more work. In a few days them little eggs hatched oot, and picked the bones o' bunny as clean as old Raq licks a plate. These young carrion beetles got their meal; the old 'uns ensured the preservation o' the race. We think it rather a nasty business. But that's one o' the ways in which the world is kept sweet and clean. It were Ned who showed me 'em at work fust of all, and he finished up wi' sayin', 'God

A'mighty thinks o' everythin', even to gettin' the menial work done'."

★   ★   ★

Jerry and I parted, but his last words, "The doin' o' menial work," remained with me. I began to look with enlightened eyes on the carrion crows and the ravens. I thought of the great army of rodents that swarm in our sewers. Then the hyenas, the jackals, the vultures passed through my mind. I thought of the blue-bottles, so trouble-some in the larder, and yet so useful in the fields. Floods and gales, frosts and swelling tides, the hunters of the living and the dead — all doing their appointed tasks and for their own ends — but as a by-product, leaving us a world where the gust of lilac breath can be appreciated, and where no taint mingles with the swaying meadow-sweet.

CHAPTER
ELEVEN

The Crested Sentinel

APRIL

It has always been an ambition of mine to photograph the plover, or lapwing as she is often called, on the nest. Jerry had promised to find one for me and also to put up my hiding-tent, so that I could snap her at close quarters.

True to his promise he sent me word that all was ready. I arrived at his cottage early in the morning for one never knows how long such an adventure may take.

"Ye've left Raq behind I see," said Jerry to me as I dumped down my paraphernalia.

I nodded. "And left him secure this time," I said, referring to the time when he eluded those at home and followed me.

"Do you want to begin at once?" Jerry asked, pointing at my camera.

"Not for an hour or so," I said, looking at my watch. "The light is none too strong yet. That putting on of the clock makes a good deal of difference you know."

"I've a nest or two ye might like to see afore we go t' plover's. It's not very far to t' tent," he said. "Could ye do wi' a bite o' summat afore we set oot?"

I shook my head. "I've had a good breakfast, thank you," I replied, "and I've a pocketful of fruit that will see me through the day."

Jerry grinned. "Ye'll not grow very fat on them, I reckon. Howsomever, every man to his fancy."

★   ★   ★

When we reached a beck which feeds the river, he took me to a small bridge. On the buttress was a large domed nest built of bents and moss. As I went nearer to it a black bird, with a splash of white on its breast, dropped out of it, and uttering a cry of "Zit-zit," winged its way with quick mechanical strokes further up the river.

"Dipper," I cried to Jerry, and putting my hand in the nest I felt five eggs.

I lifted one out very carefully and saw that it was pure white.

"No good decoratin' a thing ye can't see," was Jerry's comment, and I knew that he was alluding to the fact that the egg lay in the darkness, and was screened from view by its arched roof.

"Yon bird," said the poacher, "'as built there fer 'ears. I reckon it's the ancestral home o' them dippers and those that 'as gone afore 'em. Last year it was a'most in t' same place, and just as I got up to it, oot popped t' youngsters and flopped right doon int' watter."

"Did they swim?" I asked.

Jerry shook his head. "They did more'n that," said he. "The little beggars flopped doon in t' watter, and walked on t' bottom o' t' stream, and cam' oot t' other side."

I think I must have looked incredulous, for he continued —

"I wouldn't a believed it mysen only I seed it wi' my own eyes. O' course, I've seen the owd uns do it scores o' times. But fancy them young uns 'avin' it in 'em to start wi'. That's why the nest is allus built above t' watter, I reckon," he added.

"But it isn't always built above water," I said, and putting my hand in my pocket, I showed him a photograph I had taken a few days previously.

As Jerry scrutinized it I continued — "I was visiting a friend whose house is built by the beck-side. About ten feet from this stream is a passage — roofed in as you can see, and half-closed by a gate. That dark blob near the roof is a dipper's nest. So there's an exception to your rule," I added, with a smile.

"It only goes to prove that birds is as queer as folk," said Jerry, handing me back my snapshot. "There's oddities among 'em, just as there is among us. If them youngsters of yours which are hatched in that nest drop doon on to them flags, they'll find it harder than t' watter. There'll be some sore 'eads among 'em."

★ ★ ★

Jerry was still walking on. I halted as I thought it was time I was making for the hiding-tent, so we returned to his cottage, and having shouldered various packs, we turned our faces towards the upland meadows.

The sun was shining brilliantly, though the wind, as we mounted higher, struck rather cold.

Up a lane we wended our way, and on each side of the hedge birds were busy either searching for nesting material or for the flies and worms for which hungry mouths were waiting.

"There's the first swallow I've seen this year," I said, as a blue-black bird, with widely-forked tail, sped by.

"Turn yer money ovver fer luck then," Jerry said. "Some folks tak' it oot and spit on't as well, though I don't know what good that does."

As we turned a corner we heard the familiar cry of the plover, and a moment later the bird was flying overhead.

"There's the sentinel ye see," said my companion. "Fer sight and 'earin' I reckon them lapwings'll tak' a lot o' beatin'. He's sending doon messages to 'er on t' nest, tellin' 'er whether she's got to 'sit tight ' or else to 'hop it.' "

Then we entered the field and saw in the distance the rough sacking hiding-tent that stood near to the nest.

★　★　★

As we walked along, careful not to tread on any other eggs which might be nestling on the ground, I noticed quite a lot of holes which looked to me either like nests ready for eggs or deserted ones.

I pointed these out to Jerry. "Them are 'scrapes ' made by the cock. He mak's sometimes 'arf-a-dozen or so, so that when he's found his partner he can offer 'er a choice — and all wi' vacant possession," said he.

"It's a wonder to me," I said, as we neared the tent, "that these sheep and lambs don't walk through the nest and break all the eggs."

Jerry stood still for a moment. "They do break a goodish few," he said, "but I'll tell ye what I once saw. I were sittin' doon by a hedge, and i' the field i' front there were some plovers' nests. I could see the birds dozin' quietly on 'em. Roond about were a few sheep nibblin', and one I saw gettin' closer and closer to one o' t' nests. I thowt that i' another minnit' she'd a put 'er foot on t' sittin' bird. But just as she cam' up to it, the plover pecked 'er on't tip of 'er nose." Jerry laughed at the recollection of it. "I niver saw a more surprised owd ewe i' my life. She turned tail and skiddaddled doon t' field as though Owd Nick were after 'er. I reckon she'd be more careful where she were walkin' i' future. I've often wondered whether sheep and cattle learn to give a sittin' bird a wide berth — 'specially a plover, fer she's plucky enough to tackle a wild elephant."

★   ★   ★

At last I was safely housed in my small tent. Camera, plates, changing-bag, lenses, and my six-foot self were coiled up in three foot square. For a few hours I had to be a tabloid.

As Jerry walked away he called out, "Good luck to ye!" and I knew that as he retreated the two birds before whose nest I had camped would be watching him from some concealed position.

Three-quarters of an hour passed, and I whiled away the time of waiting by peeping through tiny spy-holes and listening to the sounds round about me. Over in the next field I could see a primary department of lambs. They were playing King-of-the-castle. Each member of the little group mounted on to a small knoll of green grass, and his other playmates then tried to butt him off his exalted position.

Farther down the field I could see that another peewit was settling comfortably down on her eggs. As Jerry and I had passed this nest I had put my head down and could distinctly hear the little birds "cheeping" inside — so the mother bird was anxious for them to break the shell — that was why she had returned as quickly as possible.

As an accompaniment I could hear blackbirds and thrushes challenging one another in song. From the hedge came the full-throated stanzas of the wren. Then the dunnock added his quick snatch of melody as though he were anxious to sing the same verse as often as possible. Above me the lark was trilling as if he were inviting earth-bound mortals to come up into the blue and see how wonderful the world looked from such eminence.

When I next looked at the nest in front of me I found that the mother-bird had stolen quietly on to it, and was gazing intently at the big eye of the lens which poked itself through the front square of my sacking.

★   ★   ★

Before I clicked the shutter and took her photograph, I gave her a chance to settle down. I then examined her carefully. What a poor description it is to describe her as black and white. On her wings is the sheen of the rainbow — purple, blue, green, give place to one another as varied shafts of light play upon them. Even her dark tail feathers are embellished with a streak of chestnut.

The full lustrous eyes have in them the tenderness of the deer's gaze, whilst the crest which can be lifted or lowered at will, sets off the dainty curve of the neck to perfection.

To test whether she was bold or timid I gently tapped my finger against the camera stand. She merely raised her crest and neck and looked fiercely at the tent.

Then I released the shutter without actually exposing a negative, just to see whether she would flinch at such a noise. I was rejoiced to see that, though it startled her, yet she merely stood up over her eggs for a moment as though debating whether she should quit or stay. However, she made up her mind that duty must be done in spite of alarms, and once more she settled down and shuffled the eggs together, making sure that her small body left no egg exposed.

And so, after a four hours' stay in the tent, and a number of hoped-for photos, I finally emerged and stretched my cramped limbs that were full of "pins and needles".

As I passed the other plover's nest I found that the wee mites were hatched, and as soon as they saw me they squatted down like statues in the nearest hole they could find. As usual the mother-bird ran in front of me, doing the broken-wing trick.

Later, when I was telling Jerry, over a cup of tea, how I had spent my time, he said — "Did ye see that someone had sent to the King a couple of the first plovers' eggs which had been found ? "

"But the taking of the eggs is illegal," I said. "The bird is such a friend to the farmers that she is protected by law."

"That's just what the King said," Jerry answered appreciatively. "He wrote to the sender tellin' him that he'd got 'em all right, but that he couldn't receive 'em. Well," here he raised his tea-cup, "here's good health to His Majesty ! "

"And also to the little bird, the friend of farmers and kings," I said, and we clinked our cups together.

CHAPTER
TWELVE

A Displenishing Sale

FEBRUARY

On our way up to the farm, I called in for a moment to see Sally Stordy. We were out earlier than usual, as the mornings were beginning to peep out with Spring light.

When she heard of our destination, she told us that Alan and Joe were going to a "'plenishing sale" which was being held at Cairn How.

"Leastways," she said, "I owerheard Alan askin' Ned what time t' bus runs to Nent End, and that's just aboot where the farm lies. I reckon that's where they'll be makin' fer to-day."

"What is a displenishing sale?" I asked, more to hear her views on such an incident than for information.

"It's a sellin' off o' everythin' that's on a farm," she answered. "Old John Laverick o' Cairn How 'as made 'is bit, I reckon. His uncle died a few years back and left 'im a goodish bit, and he's bin very careful. I never 'eard how much it were, but soon afterwards he got a car, so it must a bin a tidy sum."

She sighed as though she too wished she had an uncle.

"You may have a car of your own one day, Sally," I said. "You never know."

"That's the only car I shall ever 'ave," she answered, "and I push it mysen."

She pointed to an old perambulator which stood in a corner of the scullery.

"But John Laverick," she continued, "is gettin' beyond farmin', and he's goin' to retire. So everythin's bein' sold, lock, stock and barrel, to-day. It'll be a bit of a sad time fer him, I reckon, fer he's fond o' farmin'."

She busied herself "fettlin' up t' fireside", but hearing the sound of wheels in the street, looked out of the window.

"There's old Tom Graham off to t' sale, I'll war-want. He's a near un, I can tell ye. Hardly gives 'is missus enough to feed t' poultry, let alone t' run t' hoose, and sits there in the Chapel singin' 'Were the whole realm o' Nature mine.' It ud be a bad day fer all of us if it was his'n. When oor choir went oot carollin' at Christmas they went up to Glencarn, and —"

"Is that his farm?" I asked.

Sally nodded, and continued —

"And when they'd finished he said to his missus, 'Give 'em double this time; we've had a better year'n last,' and when old Sarah asked how much that were, he said, 'Give 'em tuppence.'"

"And what will he be going to buy?" I asked.

"Buy!" repeated Sally with a wry smile, "he'll buy nowt, I reckon, but he'll get his dinner free, and that'll just set him up fine. There'll be a big spread up there aboot eleven."

She glanced out of the window again, and added — "Why, there's Joe and Alan comin' doon. I thought they'd be goin'. I should go wi' 'em if I were you."

And so I bade her "Good-day," and joined my friends.

★ ★ ★

"Are you going to Cairn How?" I asked as I met them.

"Right first time," said Alan. "Are you comin' with us?"

When I told them that I was, Joe gave me a re-sounding thump on the back by way of emphasizing his welcome, and Raq looked at him in a puzzled kind of way, uncertain whether some bodily damage were being planned.

"I thought you went to a sale last week," I said, as we waited for the 'bus. "Are you buying up the whole district?"

"There's not much doin' this time o' the year," said Alan, referring to the farm work.

"The frost's workin' fer us," said Joe. "It pulverizes the land and sweetens it, and mak's it much easier fer the ploo and harrer to do their work later. But here's the 'bus."

My farmer friends and I entered and found it full of others who were bound for the sale. A chorus of "Morning Joe," "Mornin' Alan," greeted us, and I heard my companions reply to Tom and Abe, Dick and Harry. There are no "Mr.'s" in the countryside.

They were all talking about the grading of eggs, and I learnt that a new association was being formed whose members guaranteed to divide their supply of eggs into those weighing over and those weighing under 2 oz.

"We've not tried to compete wi' the foreigner," said one of the group ; "we're lettin' 'im send in thousands o' millions o' eggs, and all on 'em's graded. It's time we wakkened up. Us farmers are the most consarvative lot on the face o' the earth, but we'll ha' to move wi' the times."

"That's Pattison o' Fellrigg talkin'," whispered Joe to me. "He's the most up-to-date farmer in the district. Does a bit o' intensive work in grass-growin', and even has electric light fer givin' his hens more daylight i' the winter. Says it pays too."

There was a lull in the conversation as the 'bus pulled up to take in more passengers. Then a little man in the corner said —

"Talkin' aboot eggs reminds me o' the best season I ever 'ad wi' pooltry."

"Now for a yarn," Alan said quietly to me, giving me a nudge. "That's old Bill Braisby's brother, Tom, as is speakin'."

"Tha knows as ow Ah was badly troubled wi' rats," said Tom, looking round at those nearest to him. "Well,

a feller come in one day and said as 'ow he'd got two boxes o' pizun which were guaranteed to kill every rat aboot t' farm. Said he'd got 'em from some feller in t' market-place."

"Some quack, I reckon," whispered Joe to me.

"Well," continued Tom, "one neet Ah put pizun doon in an oothouse which were owerrun wi' 'em, and shut t' door. Next mornin' Ah 'ad to goa away on business, and Ah fergot to tell t' missus aboot t' pizun, and to keep t' pooltry away fra' it. Ah niver remembered owt abaht it till t' middle o' t' mornin', and then, when Ah remembered, Ah broke oot inter a cold sweeat. Ah could see all t' pooltry liggin stiff, and missus carryin' on summat awful. When Ah got 'ome, Ah went to where Ah'd put doon t' pizun, and me worst fears were confirmed, for every bit were pecked up clean as a whistle, and t' hens were waitin' roond abaht lookin' fer more."

"None dead?" asked one of his hearers.

"Not one," answered Tom. "An' after that Ah 'ad the biggest crop o' eggs Ah'd 'ad fer 'ears. Ah asked him as 'ad got me t' pizun to get two more boxes, as it were extra fer egg-prodoocin'; but he never brought 'em. So now tha knows how to git more eggs. Give 'em pizun."

Amidst general laughter the 'bus pulled up, and we found ourselves at Cairn How.

★ ★ ★

"What a crowd!" I said as I viewed the number that had gathered for the sale.

"There'll be six or seven hundred here," said Alan. "Let's go and have some dinner. It'll be in the barn up yonder. That's where they're all makin' for."

Amidst the general movement towards the scene of the lunch, little groups were gathered. As I passed, I could hear different topics of conversation. Some were discussing "foot and mouth disease." I heard others denouncing the Government. The groups maintained their numbers, but individuals would slip away and casually sidle into some other circle. So each farmer would listen to the varied broadcasting centres. Gossip, business, prices, prophecies, all centred round that sale, which became a vast watershed of news, irrigating the countryside with the thousand and one things which interest human beings.

And who can describe the dinner itself, with the plates groaning under their burden of meat and vegetables, whilst the aged rafters overhead looked on wonderingly, and the wives of the farmers of the district saw to it that your plate was never empty!

"Who pays for this?" I asked of my friends.

"The farmer whose things are bein' sold," said Alan. "I reckon it'll cost him nigh fifty pun to-day."

"But it puts 'em all in a good humour," said Joe. "Ye can't sell much to folk wi' empty stomachs. Look at old Ebb Scott ovver yonder. He don't care what becomes of 'im after this."

★ ★ ★

Now the sale is on, and the auctioneer is talking so fast that I cannot understand a word he is saying. Around him is a sea of faces, and each farmer has his own way of bidding.

Some raise a finger, others mutter that which is unintelligible to me, but the auctioneer understands and proceeds. They are selling the cattle now, and an old farmer with bushy eyebrows opposite to me just raises his left eyelid — that is his sign that he is willing to give another half-a-crown. How the auctioneer saw it, I do not know. Great must be his powers of observation.

At the back of the ring there is one bidder who when he has reached his limit tilts his bowler hat every time. The auctioneer understands the secret signal and looks elsewhere for another bid.

I left the crowd for a few moments and had a look at the varied lots. There was a binder, harrows, seed-drills, hay-bogies, a churn, a separator, carts. I saw old John Laverick having a walk round looking perchance for the last time at favourite ploughs, or on stock which had been his pride. Could any man see the dispersal of these without a heavy heart?

On my return Alan was bidding.

"What is he trying for?" I asked.

"Hoggs," said Joe to me.

"Hogs?" I asked with surprise. "But you've got as many pigs as you can manage."

Joe laughed.

"The Hoggs is a kind o' sheep," he answered.

I was completely mystified as I listened to the talk round about me. I knew there were ewes and tups, but after that all the rest were "sheep " to me.

But I heard men speaking of gimmers, shearlings, hoggs, wethers. Then, amongst cattle, there were cows, bulls, stirks, heifers, bullocks, polled and unpolled.

Joe laughed when I told him of this mystifying vocabulary, and said —

"Now you know how some on us feel when you parsons use some o' your own special brand i' the pulpit."

My friend said it humorously, but I felt there was a great deal of truth in what he said.

"How's the sale going off?" I asked Alan quietly.

"Oh, nobbet middlin'. Beasts are not sellin' well. Fodder's ower scarce!"

★ ★ ★

At last everything had been disposed of. The hammer, devoid of all sentiment, had scattered the effects of John Laverick to the four winds. The bidders, thinking the sale was over, were turning to go homewards, when the auctioneer called their attention to the last lot.

Alan pulled my sleeve, and I saw in the ring a black and white sheep dog. It was slender of limb, and reminded me of a cross-bred collie.

It was led in by a string, and looked pathetically out of place. I did not like the look in its quiet brown eyes.

"This is the last sale," whispered Alan. "It's a fine dog, too."

As the auctioneer was describing its virtues, some one came and stood by me. I turned and saw that it was the old farmer to whom the dog belonged.

As though some secret message had flashed to the dog, it raised its eyes and saw him, straightened itself slightly, and then slowly wagged its tail. There was nothing joyous in the motion, just the recognition of affection.

For a moment I thought the old man was going to buy the dog in. But he changed his mind, and, as the bidding commenced, with an effort turned away.

LOT
369

The chatter continued all around me. After all, to most of them there, men were only bidding for a dog. After seeing Laverick, I rather fancied they were buying a bit of the old farmer's heart.

"Who got him?" asked Joe of his brother.

"Brownlea of Fellstone," answered Alan. "He'll mak' a good master for 'im."

As we made our way to the 'bus we went over to Laverick and bade him Good-day.

"By the way," I said to him, "why didn't you keep that dog of yours?"

He was silent for a moment, and then said —

"'Twouldn't be fair," said he. "He lives fer the sheep, and I'm a-goin' to live in the toon."

Then I understood.

CHAPTER
THIRTEEN

Kestrel Ledge

JUNE

At this time of the year I always know where to find John Fell, the gamekeeper. He is watching his young pheasants in the field where numerous coops hold his "silkies." These are an excellent type of broody hen used as foster-mothers.

Leaving Raq outside the enclosed land, I walked over to his hut, where he was busy mixing food for his big family.

"And how are your young pheasants coming on?" I asked.

"Fine," he said; "the dry weather suits 'em better than the wet."

"Had many losses?" I asked.

"A few," he answered. "The crows are very hungry fer 'em, and ye've got to keep yer eyes skinned fer any hawks that tak' a fancy fer young game."

"Pampered darlings," I said, referring to the artificial protection which was meted out to these fancied youngsters.

"Aye," said he, shaking his head, "and we pay too big a price fer the preservation of these and a few others."

I knew what he meant, though naturally he spoke about such things with reserve. He loved every wild thing. As he was silent, I put into words his own thoughts —

"Just because a comparatively small number of the community want the pleasure of shooting game, every enemy of it has to be exterminated — stoats, weasels, polecats, hawks of all kinds, buzzards and kites, harriers, ravens, and owls — all have to go."

As he came out of the hut a wood-pigeon flew up into one of the trees at the edge of the field.

"Have you ever noticed how numerous they are becomin'?" he asked.

I nodded. "So numerous that 'shoots' are now being organized in many districts to thin down their numbers."

"That's so," said John. "I'm allus tellin' ye, ye can't upset the balance o' Natur'. Ye kill the hawks and the 'cushat' (wood-pigeon) escapes. The sportsmen get their pheasants, and the farmers are owerrun by pigeons. An onnateral raisin' o' one breed means an onnateral killin' o' another, and atween the two, summat that oughtn't gits the benefit."

"By the way," I said, "I heard that you had a kestrel's nest that you were keeping to show me. Have you time to go to-day?"

John consulted his watch. "I'll just give these coops a drop or two o' water, and then Ben (the under-keeper)

106

should be here. If ye like to have a ratch round fer an hour by yersel', I'll be ready fer ye."

* * *

Raq looked rather reproachfully at me as I released him, but the wag of his tail showed that his forgiveness was a very complete one.

"We're on our own for a short time, old man," I said to him. "Let's take it easily and potter round just to see what we can find. Shall we go down to the river?"

Now, whether he understood all I said is questionable. He loved the tone in which I spoke and knew that its omens were good. Also he knew what the sound "river' meant. Whenever I spoke it, there followed a visit to the running water which he loved. So when I mentioned it again, his whole body wriggled with delight. "Carried unanimously" wagged his tail.

Along its banks veiled with trees and swaying grasses, we proceeded slowly. I almost put my foot upon a little whitethroat's nest. From under my boot a midget bird with a light throat and grey-brown back fluttered on to a neighbouring spray of meadow-sweet, which curved as though it would break under its dainty burden.

Then in a little nest, screened by the mosses of the bank, I saw six small white eggs with scarlet spots dappling them.

I retreated from the feathery home but a few yards, and the little mother, in no wise afraid, fluttered back on to a blackberry trailer, peeped at her nest to see that

all was secure, and then popped in to continue her incubating.

As the dog scrambled along I saw a different bird leave the bank, and as soon as she reached the shingle, she immediately began to do the broken wing trick. Raq, of course, saw her as she meant him to do, and was lured far from the nest she had left in the bank.

There I found her four light brown eggs with their rich dark brown markings.

When the dog returned from his vain chase, we hid ourselves, but no bird returned to the nest.

Here were two nests within a few yards of each other, but what different temperaments the owners possessed! How differently, too, the nests were built! One, the sandpiper's, rested in a "scrape' on the bank, and was lined with bents and dried grasses — a very ordinary affair. "Peggy whitethroat's" was a tender little home of moss, hair and feathers, cosily tucked under the grass thatch of the top of the bank.

For a short time a heavy shower began to fall. Lovely music the big drops made on the outspread leaves. Only a few moments before the leaves were green, with a "matt" surface. Now each one glistened like a mirror, and as the sun shone through the cloud, the leaves reflected the blue sky — shimmering green and blue on each leaf — and behind in the shadow stood the dark trunk with soft tones of grey, purple, green and black. What a glorious world!

As the rain fell in great drops the gnats still kept up their endless dance. How in the world do they manage to fly in the rain? One drop, if it struck them, is enough to dash them to the wet earth. One drop is enough to bedraggle those wings of gossamer lace. And yet this tiny wisp of dancing life defies the shower!

I wonder, yes, I wonder, whether the big drop in its rush to the ground creates such a draught that it wafts the little midge out of its track. I am still wondering. I wish I could be certain.

★   ★   ★

When we returned to the field of the young pheasants, John was ready to accompany us.

"Is it far?" I asked.

"Three miles mebbee, up on the fell," he answered.

"That means nearly five miles," I said, turning to the dog. "We've had some of John's arithmetic before, haven't we, old man?"

John smiled, and I said, "Did you say that there were young hawks in the nest we're going to?"

The keeper nodded.

"And are you going to destroy them eventually?" I asked, knowing that many keepers complain of the kestrel's damage to young game birds.

"No," said John decisively; "the only time I shoot a kestrel is when I find him deliberately visitin' the young chicks and makin' off wi' 'em. As a rule, ye'll find that a bird which raids coops has a nest full o' young uns not so very far away. Then's the time ye've got to stop a wild freebooter like that." He was silent for a moment or two, and we plodded quietly along our upward climb. "I'm sorry fer 'em too, fer they're only doin' what all on us does."

"Getting our living along the line of least resistance, eh? Finding our food with the least amount of fag," I explained.

"That's it now," said my companion. "Good mornin', Dave," said he to an old shepherd, who was following his sheep up the hillside. "What's the weather goin' to turn oot?"

The old man rested on his stick, whistled shrilly to his dog to lie down, and surveyed the sky as slowly and thoroughly as though he were looking at it for the first time in his life.

"I don't like the looks on't," said he, and, after learning whither we were going, said, "Well, don't go along Thorsfell Ridge — there's mist comin', and ye might be up there the night."

"Shall I offer him a bit of tobacco?" I whispered to John.

"Not on your life," said he to me, whilst a note of fear crept into his voice. "He calls them the instruments o' the devil, and we'll never get to the nest if once ye mak' him let loose on pipes and sich like."

* * *

Now our walking became more difficult. A stiff climb would take us to the top of a ridge only to discover that between us and the next height lay a deep ghyll. In this all was peace and quietness. The wild pansies smiled at us with their yellow open faces, though the little blue speedwells closed themselves for security as though emphasizing the shepherd's warning. Amongst the rocks a grey, white and black bird, with a dark stripe running from the bill through the eye, curtsied and flitted with jerky flight from stone to stone. I looked at my companion.

"Wheatear," said he; "that yaller-tinted breast goes well wi' that grey, don't it? A dapper little gentleman," he added, as we watched it dart in and out of several hiding-places.

"Shall we find his nest in one of those holes in the stones?" I asked, eager to find the bird's domicile.

John shook his head. "He's foolin' ye," said he. "He'll dart into a score o' places. But ye'll be a lucky un if ye come across it easily." We plodded on. "Must be a great change from Africa's sun to a wild place like this," he added, alluding to the annual migration of this bird.

Then, as we neared our final climb, John touched my arm and pointed upwards. At first I could not see anything. At last, hundreds of feet up, I saw a dark speck.

"Kestrel," said John.

I brought my field-glasses to bear on it, and for a moment or two the hawk, head to the wind, seemed to be suspended motionless in mid-air. A far-away cry full of solitude and solicitude trailed down to us. "Kele" — then a pause — "Kelee.' Lonesome it sounded, yet it caught the very spirit of the crag and glen.

"She's watchin' us now that we're getting near the nest," said John.

"Near the nest, are we?" I repeated, wiping the perspiration from my brow. "We're glad to hear of it, aren't we, old man?" I said, turning to the dog.

And in order to enhearten me, my companion pointed to a shoulder of rocks about a quarter of a mile ahead. "It's yonder," he said.

★   ★   ★

At last I looked up at the ledge where the young ones lay. The "whitewash" on its rim and down the face of the rock advertised their presence. The youngsters were shouting out for food.

I found a foothold which enabled me to reach up into the nest with one hand, but I hastily withdrew it. I had been used to handling young birds with impunity. These young hawks resented my intrusion and promptly fastened their claws in my fingers.

"Shakin' hands wi' ye, are they?" laughed John from below, as he saw the quick withdrawal and the surprised look on my face.

I drew myself up still further, and then I saw those I had climbed far to see.

"They're aboot sixteen hundred feet up," said John, as I gazed at six little fluffy furies who were ever ready

to turn on their backs and bring their yellow talons into a fighting attitude.

As the keeper saw me watching them he said, "They're ready fer givin' ye a straight left, I reckon?"

I nodded. "And they are handy with their grey curved beaks too," I said, sucking one of my fingers.

Then, before I got my camera to work, I examined their eyrie.

A flat ledge of rock was the nesting site. There was only the scantiest of nesting material, and the odour was not that of Araby. Brown feathers from the breast of some small bird told of their menu. I threw some down to John, and he said, "Titlark." Then I picked out a skull which still possessed a blunt, rounded nose of fur. "Field-vole," I heard John say, as he examined it.

I fixed the camera in position and carried away with me something of the fierceness of those rounded liquid eyes — full of flame, glinty flame. A hard life lay before them, but no fear or yellow streak lurked in those bold orbs. Very soon, too, instead of that silken down, would be chestnut-tinted wings that would learn how to swoop on prey shivering in the grass, or to poise a slender body motionless in a breezy sky.

Young thrushes in the nest call forth my sympathy, the feathery wisps of life in the tit's hole touch some tender chord within. But the young hawks thrill me

113

with the sense of adventure, and send me forth to face the world with a more dauntless courage. The secret lies in their eyes.

★ ★ ★

Not far from the hawk's nest a bird not unlike a blackbird flew near us with some concern.

"Ring-ousel," said John. "See the white crescent on its breast?"

"It squawks like a starling," I said.

"And pipes like an angel when it's a mind to," said he; "a clear ringin' flute speakin' o' joy and content."

He bent down and called me to look at a hole in a broken-down wall. There lay four little embryo songsters in a nest not unlike the blackbird's.

"Why," I said, "that kestrel can see them when she's on her own ledge. Why doesn't she use them up for her hungry young?"

"That's one o' the mysteries," said John. "Things that live handy to 'em they seem to leave alone. 'Live and let live' may be their motter fer their near neighbours."

And so we set our faces homewards. The rain lashed us with fury, and the wind tried to stem our descent. But what odds! Had I not seen the raiders in their lair, and perchance caught something of their indomitable courage?

Many times, too, shall I, when hemmed in by streets and house-fronts, let my inner eye look upwards toward the blue, and see in imagination the mother kestrel, now circling, now motionless, in the larger air. Even the vision of that will tend to lift me out of the routine shackles of every day, and for a few moments I shall hear the "Ke-lee" of the wider sky.

CHAPTER
FOURTEEN

The Night Vigil

AUGUST

It was good to see Jerry again, and by the gleam in his eyes I knew that he had a welcome for Raq and me.

"Ye're lookin' rare well," said he; "as brown as a berry. I reckon that caravan life suits ye."

I went over to him and felt the muscles of his arms.

"I do believe you have been doing some work," I said, whilst Raq sniffed round his leggings and sorted out the varied scents which still clung to them.

He laughed. "Just a bit o' harvestin' fer Alan and Joe," said he. "But I've got to be careful not to owerdo it, ye know."

We pulled out our pipes and sat on the grass that fringed the outside of his cottage.

"Did John Fell ask you to take a night for him to guard his young pheasants?" I asked.

"Quite a few," answered Jerry.

"Did anything interesting turn up?" I queried.

"Well," said my companion, blowing out great puffs of smoke, "there was one old dog-fox rather persistent-like."

I settled myself comfortably to hear the story.

"Ye know the hut where John stops?" he asked.

I nodded. "Right in the middle of the big spinney," I answered.

"I got down there," Jerry continued, "and as dusk came on, one by one the young pheasants went nicely up into the pines to roost. The old cocks as they went into the branches sang out their hoarse challenge (they like to let every one know that it's bed-time, ye know). Everything, as I had a last walk roond, were peaceful and content."

In my mind's eye I was visualizing the scene — the great masses of the pines in one thick shadow, the "ride" which divided them almost light in comparison with their indigo depth. Still night, save for some bird giving itself a final preen before settling down to sleep, or a fleeting glance of a white moth as the light of the stars fell upon its silken sails. Above the ground — the world of wing asleep; on the ground — the thickets slightly moving as some unseen hunter followed an enticing trail.

"Then, after a bit," I heard my companion saying, "there seemed to be a stir amongst the roosting birds. Once, I heard one of 'em call oot i' fear. The restlessness were like a wave. It touched a belt o' trees and were gone. Then as I walked oot to see what was the cause on't, it 'ud wakken up agin i' some other part o' t' wood."

117

He pulled meditatively at his pipe, Raq watching his every movement and gazing at him as though he were following every word.

"I visited the lamps to see that they were all right, but when I had a look roond as dawn were breakin', I saw an old fox slinkin' away ower a hill that leads to t' fells. 'So you're the varmint that's disturbin' the peace, are ye?' I thowt."

"The lamps are for frightening off foxes, aren't they?" I asked.

Jerry nodded. "The light frightens 'em fer a time," said he, "but they get used to 'em. I reckon it 'ud tak' a movin' searchlight to scare away a determined hungry un."

"And had he got any of the pheasants?" I asked anxiously.

"Not as far as I could see," said Jerry, "but he badly skeered 'em. How 'ud you like to be sittin' up i' the branches on a dark night and oppen yer eyes to see two green balls o' flame shinin' up at ye?"

"I should sit tight, knowing that he couldn't climb the tree. I should probably pull faces at him," I said.

"But what if them eyes kind o' hypnotized ye, and started pullin' ye doon wi' invisible wires, eh?" asked Jerry earnestly.

"A fox can't do that, surely," I said, disbelievingly.

"Well, how does he get 'em doon to t' ground then?" asked the old poacher.

"Oh," said I, "when you find a bird a fox has killed, it has been an odd one that decided to roost either low down or under some bush."

118

"Ye've that to tak' into accoont o' course," said he, "but when all's bin said on them groonds, ye've still to find oot how they tice 'em doon from t' branches higher up."

★ ★ ★

"And is that the end of the story?" I asked, as Jerry did not seem to be too eager to continue.

"No," said he, "that sort o' thing happened agin and agin when I was on dooty, so I had a word wi' John aboot it, and then slipped doon to old Simeon Boswell's camp. What e' don't know aboot foxes ain't worth knowin'."

"Or pheasants," said I, smiling.

"I told him what had happened, and he whistled up old Boz and spoke to him like a Christian fer a few minutes — said something aboot 'Chiriklos in the wesh' — and the dog followed me like a lamb."

"Pheasants in the wood," said I, interpreting the Romany words.

"Well," continued he, "the dog and me went to the hut and I thowt we were in fer a quiet night. Suddenly I heerd the first stir amongst the birds, so I went outside wi' Boz."

He paused for a moment, rose and acted the whole scene before me.

"The dog pricked up his ears, then up went his nose, and I could see the fur roond his neck risin' like a stiff brush — but never a sound fell from his lips. He gave me one inquirin' look and I patted him. 'Good dorg,'

said I, and the old fellow, with me behind him, led towards where the birds were bein' skeered.

"I soon lost him i' the darkness. Then I heard a big snarl, and the sound of a body hurling itself through the brushwood — then silence."

"He'd found the fox all right?" I said.

Jerry nodded. "I stood where I was fer some minutes, whilst only the owls hooted owerhead. Then, away on the fringe o' the wood, there come the sound o' another skirmish, and I heard no more till Boz returned and nosed me oot, with his tongue lolling oot, and a look i' his eyes which said, 'We've bin 'avin' a 'igh old time.'"

"Did he get the fox?" I asked eagerly.

"Only a bit of 'im," said my friend. "There were a bunch o' red fur hangin' on to the side o' his jaws, and old Reynard took away a bit o' Boz's left ear as a souvenir o' their meetin' — but there were no more skeerin' o' pheasants i' that wood."

"Old Boz must have done a bit of skilful stalking to get on to the fox as well as he did," I said.

120

"Aye, you bet he did" — and then Jerry gave one of his delightful chuckles. I love to hear them. They are like bubbling springs, and somehow or other join up with one's own inner ripples.

"What's the joke?" I asked.

"Oh," he laughed, "when I think o' the old gipsy's dog defendin' John's pheasants while he hisself is asleep i' bed and —"

"Jerry the poacher leadin' the attack," I interpolated.

"It's enough to mak' a cat laugh," said he.

★　★　★

After finishing our pipes, Jerry asked me whether I had ever seen a badger.

"Not very often," I answered.

"We'll walk up and see his 'sett', if ye like. I caught sight of old Brock sneakin' back to his den i' the early mornin' hours, as I were returnin' to the hut. I rather fancy he had bin takkin' his young family oot fer their suppers."

As we walked along the lane towards the wood which Jerry had pointed out, he called my attention to the swallows resting on the barn of the farm.

"That's a sign that autumn is on us. It looks as though they've called a meetin' to settle the route they'll tak' to the South."

I listened to the twittering, low and fully enunciated. It sounded as though the birds were, as Jerry said, discussing the details of their long flight.

Soon we were in the wood, and the dog stood sniffing outside what looked like an enlarged rabbit-hole.

"That's where old 'Silver Muzzle' enters," said my companion.

"Anyone might think that it was only the entrance to a large warren," I said.

"Not wi' such a pad mark as yon," said Jerry, pointing to a five-toed impression in the soft sand. "Look at the strong marks o' the claws. Rabbits only leave little pin-point pricks behind 'em. The paws that made them tracks are the finest spades i' the world. But get doon

on yer knees and see if ye can find anything else."

I did as my friend asked, and after searching at the entrance, came across two tell-tale silver hairs. "That settles it," said I, and looking down its dark depths, I asked, "I wonder how big the burrow is?"

Jerry thought for a moment, and then answered, "Tak' a walk fer a hundred yards straight on, and then tak' a turn to the right fer fifty or sixty more. Even then I reckon ye won't a' covered it."

I looked at him incredulously.

"There's bin badgers here fer scores o' years," he said.

"You never see much of them," said I.

"No," continued my friend, "an' if ye'd been hunted wi' terriers, and shut up i' small boxes and made to fight fer yer life, and when ye recovered from yer wounds made to fight agin until at last ye pegged oot wi' weakness — ye'd not show yerself abroad very much. But for all that, there are far more badgers aboot than folks know of, and year after year they enlarge their burrows till nobody knows how big they are."

I walked on a little way, and found Raq scratching out a rabbit-hole. He was tearing away the roots with his teeth, digging with his front paws, and kicking out the loosened soil with quick strokes of his hind legs.

"There must be a rabbit or two in there," I said, bringing Jerry to the spot. "What if, as they burrow down, they strike the badger's corridors? Will 'Brocky' drive them out?"

Jerry shook his head. "That badger's 'sett' is so big that it'll hold not only a rabbit family, but in another part of it I've known a fox to live. I don't suppose that if they lived i' the same flat they would ever run up agin one another, but —"

Here he paused such a long time that I said, "Well?"

"Ye know that a badger is a very clean animal, don't ye?"

I nodded.

"Well," said Jerry slowly, "if I were a badger and a fox lived wi'in fifty yards o' me, I should order quarts o' Eau de Cologne — but p'raps he likes it."

"One man's meat is another man's poison, you know," I said.

"Aye," said Jerry, "and p'raps a fox's stench is a badger's fragrance. It's a queer world and no mistake."

CHAPTER
FIFTEEN

On Keeping an Even Keel

JANUARY

The other morning as I sat in my study I heard a ring at the bell. Then I listened to some kind soul telling my wife that she had brought her a pot of home-made marmalade which she would like her to try. "You'll find it on the stiff side," Mrs. Jenkins had remarked as she left; "my family prefer it like that."

To me this sounded strangely reminiscent of Mrs. Jones's parting words as she put a pot of marmalade in my wife's hands as we left her house. "You'll find it rather syrupy, but we prefer it like that. It's home-made, so you do know what's in it."

How many times have I been "out to tea" and before me has lain a splendid array of dainty cakes. My heart has been set on tasting a certain dish, but before I could state my preference, like a death-knell to all my hopes, my hostess has said, "Try these, they are home-made, you know." On tasting them that has been only too self-evident!!! "There is nothing quite like home-made," I have murmured with my eyes on the other dish, and inwardly adding, "Thank goodness!"

Strange it is, how women will boast of cakes and jams that are home-made, yet will try to hide the fact that their frocks are home-made too. Strange, too, is the custom of depositing sample pots of marmalade in the houses of one's friends. No one ever leaves a rice pudding or a jam roly-poly, though these are home-made too. I wonder why?

I think it must have been these gifts of marmalade that reminded my wife to try also, for one morning on

entering the kitchen I saw a formidable array of empty pots on the table. She, too, was about to demonstrate the superiority of her recipe.

"We are going to make some marmalade," she said to me, giving a final polish to a huge brass pan.

"Is it to be of the stiff or the loose variety — rallentando on the plate or allegretto?" I asked gravely. "Or don't you decide which you prefer until you see how it turns out?"

I rather think that this last remark of mine gave her the impression that I was a hostile witness, and she refused to be communicative.

The manufacture of the marmalade has gone on, with spurts of feverish energy and with hours of unwonted calm. The oranges and lemons, I understand, will not fraternize unless reduced to infinitesimal shreds. These stand in water in the brass pan for twenty-four hours, and the aroma in the house at first is fragrant. It becomes more pronounced when at the end of that time the still is placed on the gas-cooker. The study reeks with it. The bedrooms are steeped in it.

Then the sugar has to be weighed and added, and once more the house has the odour of a toffee factory. Smell and stickiness are now everywhere. My wife is sticky, the maid is sticky, the little girl is like a fly-paper.

Sample saucerfuls are now placed on the step outside the kitchen door to see whether it will "jelly" — that is how Raq became sticky and how several samples disappeared.

"Do keep Raq out of our way," my wife said plaintively.

It was at this point of the proceedings that I felt I ought to consult John Rubb on a matter of urgent business.

As we left the house my wife thrust a pot of marmalade in my arms. "Leave that for Sally as you pass; I promised her a jar, and keep it right side up."

★　★　★

When we reached the shop I saw that the old Ford was standing before it. I thought at first that John must be going out to see whether he could get a salmon, but I saw no fishing-tackle in it.

"Thought I'd run out to the Metal Bridge," said he, "to have a look at the river. Can you spare an hour or so?"

"Nothing I should like better," said I heartily.

In a few minutes we were threading our way out of the town.

"This is the last ride you'll have in her," said John, patting the steering-wheel, and with a note of genuine regret in his voice.

"I'm sorry," I said in the same tone. "Our outings won't feel the same in a new 'bus — she's been part of the fun."

"I've got a sort of affection for the old Tin-Lizzie too," said he, and relapsed into silence.

I had too. She had carried us through sunshine and storm. We had left her standing in soaking lanes and sodden woods. She had throbbed her way over stubble fields, and her back seat had known the touch of pheasant and partridge, grouse and snipe, hares and salmon. She had scars on her, it is true, and every one spoke of some adventure. She had sunk into ditches, waded fords, tried conclusions with gate-posts — but she had never let us down. True, she had her own way of protesting — but that was only when we forgot to put water in the radiator, or thought that oil was too much of a luxury for her. Still, we forgave her these idiosyncrasies.

"Aye," said John, "the missus says that's she's a perfect disgrace, and that she won't ride in her again. I've kept putting her off, but women are queer fish. They're like a weasel on the trail. They get an idea into their heads, and you think they've forgotten it when they don't mention it. Then it pops up again. 'The Jollinses have got a new car, I see,' she said to me a week ago. And yesterday she said, 'I see that our neighbours have a new Morris.' I know what that means. What another woman has, every woman wants. So I've ordered a Morris. It'll save a lot o' natterin' in the long run. Mind you, we'd never quarrel over it, but she'd mention it whenever we saw a nice new-looking car on the road."

"That is what is meant by peaceful penetration," I said, as we drew up by the side of the road and saw the river winding like a snake in front of us.

★   ★   ★

We walked on to the bridge and gazed down on the clear water beneath. How beautiful the stones appeared over which it glided! Every colour was enhanced and polished. Pink and blue, topaz and sapphire, looked up at us from the shallows.

"There's a fine fish," said John, pointing out to me a dark green back that lay like a submarine in the gentle current.

"Always nose up stream," I said.

129

"Aye," said my companion, "if they were to turn round the other way they'd drown. Even when they return to the estuary they go back the best bit o' the way tail fust. If they didn't the water would get behind their gills and choke 'em."

Further down the river a fish suddenly launched itself into the air. Like a moonbeam it flashed in the pearly light, a bow of shimmering silver, then plunged into the pool with a resounding splash.

"I wonder what makes them do that?" I said.

John shook his head. "Can't say," he answered. "They don't feed on anything after they leave the sea — so it's not like a trout springing after a fly. Some say that it rids 'em of the sea-lice — little round spots o' black jelly they look like. But I think that they jump just for the joy o' life that's in 'em. Lambs skip about in spring, and hares have a mad frolic in the fields, so why shouldn't a salmon do a river-dance if he wants to, eh?"

We left the bridge and found our way on to the river bank. Here Raq was in his element, and the waterhens gave him elusive sport. Across the river rabbits disported themselves in the sunshine. Their burrows were high up in the river bank. Quite contentedly they watched the dog, making no effort to hide — they knew that they were safe with the river between them. Raq, too, saw them and stood quite still at the water's edge as though debating whether he should cross and introduce himself.

Finally, he decided to pay them a visit. The rabbits unconcernedly saw him take to the water. Not one of

130

them stirred, yet I could see that they were watching his movements very carefully.

When in mid-stream one of them sat bolt upright, ears erect. For a moment longer he kept his eyes fixed on the dog, then eased himself to a sitting position. Still the other rabbits showed no sign of alarm. Now the dog was within four yards of the bank, no doubt congratulating himself on getting so near to his victims. Suddenly the sentinel buck gave a thud on the earth with his strong hind leg. For a moment there was a commotion of moving brown forms, a flash or two of vanishing tails, and then the dog raced up the bank to find himself the only living thing to be seen.

He sniffed at half-a-dozen holes in the vain hope of finding something to chase, and then, at my whistle, paddled back again across the stream.

★ ★ ★

Further on we found a still pool, and in a sheltered spot we sat down and watched the minnows dance in the shallows. Once a big trout sailed by, and the minnows darted into the shallow creeks where the thinness of the water prevented the big dreadnought from following.

"We shall be able to fish in a month or so — thank goodness the 'close' season will be over," said John, nodding at the big fellow as he shot into deeper water. Then, having lit his pipe, he added, "Ever think we owe a big debt of gratitude to fish?"

131

As I did not answer, John proceeded, "They were the first livin' things to swim on an even keel — the first things to know what right-side-upness means."

I still fixed my gaze on the water, fascinated by the sinuous, graceful movements of everything which swam in it.

"Aye," said John musingly, "Nature found a winner in the fish. All around her were clams, jelly-fish, and oysters. Then she hit on the idea of enclosing a brain in a gristly box, gave a spinal column which radiated scaffoldin' on which solid flesh could be built, and put an organ in its head which told it when it was on its back or on its side."

"You mean she built her first ship," I said with growing interest.

John nodded. "And gave it a kind o' gyroscope within its ear which gives it a sense o' balance. No one will ever know how difficult it was for things in the water to keep their heads up-stream, or to swim in the right position. No one will ever know how often those early adventurers of millions o' years ago side-slipped, or swerved, or found themselves on their backs when they wanted to be on their fronts. But the time came when that wonderful balancing instrument in the ear changed all that, and then, when that came into being, everything was plain sailin', or swimmin' — but a fish was the first thing in the world to use it." He looked at me with a smile and added, "You're lookin' a bit doubtful."

"Well," I said, "it's rather hard to believe that a fish has passed this on to all living creatures."

"It's true enough," John said, "and even though we've got the instrument in our own ears, yet we've got to practise with it before it becomes perfect — those children of yours had many a fall before they could walk upright. Think of what happens when you first learn to ride a bicycle."

John looked at his watch. "Time we were getting back, I think. I told them at the shop I shouldn't be long."

★　★　★

As I left John at his shop I turned away from the old Ford feeling that I would like to have expressed my feelings of gratitude to it.

Then my mind turned to the subject of our talk. When I was a boy it was quite a common thing to see a perspiring man propping up some sagging female who was trying to master the intricacies of riding on two wheels. What an epic could be written on the theme — "The man who taught his wife to ride!" How different that lissom creature who skimmed the ground like a fairy must have felt to him when, at an angle of forty-five degrees, she deposited her eight stones of female loveliness into masculine arms, one of which held the saddle, whilst the other gripped the handlebars!

But such sights are things of the past. Probably the children of to-day learn the art of balance in early years. Soon after they can toddle they are presented with a scooter, and the little organ in the ear teaches them to adapt themselves. After that, an ordinary cycle, or even a motor-cycle, has no terrors for them.

Half-way home I looked up and stood gazing at a blue tit feeding topsy-turvy in the trees.

I was wondering at its perfect balance, when suddenly I skidded on a piece of orange-peel. "My gyroscope," I said to the dog who gravely watched my contortions as I regained my normal position, "is —"

But I never finished my sentence, for as I kicked the offending peel into the gutter, it reminded me of the marmalade which I ought to have given to Sally, and which still rested in the back of the old Ford.

"Pray heaven," I murmured as we retraced our steps, "that the marmalade has not lost its secret of right-side-upness."

When we reached the old 'bus, we found, alas! a golden stream of stickiness running in all directions.

"I'll have to tell your mistress," I said grimly, "that her marmalade is distinctly *allegretto*."

CHAPTER SIXTEEN

On Buying Lambs

MAY

"Green England" was the phrase that fell from my lips as the dog and I walked over the fields. And yet how poor it is to describe the Spring beauty! Looking at the growing grass, and using it as a standard colour, how varying is the shade which we call green! There is the tender sap-green of the chestnut, and the darker grey-green of the elm. The holly looks sombre against the yellow-green of the new leaves of the oak — there are hundreds of varying greens.

What a beautiful mosaic the fields of England must present to the lark which soars high over-head — the flaming lemon of the charlock, the deep gold of the buttercups, the light magenta of clover, the purple brown of the clean earth, all framed in the white beading of may-blossom.

By the beck we sat down and listened to its gurgles and its tinkling laughter. No wonder David's harp charmed the evil spirit from Saul. Even so does the music of running water banish the blight of city life.

CURLEW ON THE NEST

At such times of indolence I like to listen to the natural voices round about me. Not far away a curlew bubbled out its song, joyful that its youngsters were safe and sound in the fields. In the grass the grasshopper fizzed and scraped, and at times I heard the needle-like challenge of some tiny shrew. Then a big blundering bumble-bee came near and played a heavy trombone solo as he fell on some open flower. "Zit-zit," cried the kingfisher as it flitted by. "Bee-r, — Be-eer," finished off the greenfinch. Just to round the beauty of it all, a pied wagtail appeared on the shingle and tripped with mincing steps and flicking tail. What an orchestra played whilst it danced its tiny "two-step"!

I looked down at Raq. He had his eyes half-closed, but his nose kept twitching. His friend is the breeze which brings him tidings of what lurks in the bush and grass. The same scene which thrills and quietens me is before him. How differently we react to it — and yet our appreciation of natural beauty is, comparatively speaking, of recent growth!

★　★　★

We climbed up the hill which leads from the beck to the farm. Soon the sounds which we heard were very different from those down in the glen. There was the cackle of hens and the satisfied grunt of sleeping pigs. In the distance a cow was calling for the calf which was not allowed to run with her. Swallows were "chittering" as they dashed into the open door of the barn, whilst the old goose and gander stretched out long necks, and, looking at you with inflamed eyes, hissed like serpents.

Up the track which leads to the farm I saw a stranger making his way. By his side trotted a black-and-white sheep-dog, and in a moment or two the barking of the farm dogs, interspersed with a few snarls and growls, told me that he was at the kitchen door.

A few minutes later when I arrived I found him drawn up to the table with Alan and Joe having the proverbial "ten o'clock."

★ ★ ★

Charlotte had told me as I passed through the scullery that "Dick Whitley were here, after buying some lambs I reckon," but no one would have dreamed that such was his business by listening to the conversation. Yet every one around that table knew why he had come.

They talked about the weather, and agreed that a "good sup o' rain" would do the crops good. Dick related what he had seen various farmers doing as he had crossed their lands — Whiterigg was cleaning out his ditches, and Red Dyke was "fettlin' up" his gates and hedges. No reference whatever was made to the fact that he himself had come up to the farm to buy lambs. This main business seemed to me to be put deliberately into the background, yet each party knew

137

that in a few moments it would be the centre of interest.

How differently I should have proceeded had I been the buyer! I should have walked up to the farm, and, having found Joe, I should have begun at once by saying, "Good morning, Joe. Have you any lambs for sale, and if so what are you asking for them?"

But that is the direct method of the city, and is not the way of the tillers of the soil. Theirs is more leisurely, but none the less sure.

We of the town delight in making frontal attacks, but those of the land walk quietly round their Jericho, without sound or fuss until the walls fall down flat.

Such I saw was to be the strategy of the morning, for, after the "ten o'clock" was over, each drew out his pipe and filled it to the brim. Such a sign told me that the selling and buying of lambs was not going to be a quick incident — it was going to have all the elements of a campaign.

Finally, when the pipes were well lit, without a word being said, we all filed out into the yard and drifted towards the pen in which a few lambs bleated out their dissatisfaction.

When the pen was reached it was interesting to watch the movements of the interested parties. Joe leaned up against the wall, Alan sat down on the edge of a water-trough, and Dick looked quietly at the lambs, at the same time straddling out his legs and pushing back his cap from off his forehead.

Neither Alan nor Joe took any notice of him. They were gazing abstractedly, the one at the distant hills, the other at the ground immediately in front of him. Dick's dog lay at his feet with his nose between his paws — he had evidently witnessed many such scenes and knew the ritual by heart.

Finally, after Dick had gazed at them long and earnestly and had made up his mind that they really were lambs and not hyenas or giraffes, he climbed over into the pens for a closer inspection.

It was at this moment that my two farm friends stirred with new life. The struggle was about to start — the seconds were out of the ring, and both parties were about to spar for an opening. They leaned over the pen and puffed vigorously at their pipes, each suck being distinctly given, each suck saying to Dick, who was feeling the youngsters, "There's lambs fer ye — finest i' the district"; whilst across the countenance of the buyer there flitted a look of disappointment, even of gloom.

Now had I been buying a lamb I should have used very different tactics from Dick. I should have lifted it by the shoulders to see whether its front legs were straight, and have run my hands down its neck and spine and pressed firmly on its hind quarters, as the judges do at dog shows. I should have looked at its teeth and the expression in its eyes. Probably, too, I should have felt its breast-bone, even as one feels the breast of a chicken to see whether it be plump.

Dick, however, placed one hand firmly on its back and pressed evenly, steadily, at the same time looking as serious as though he were settling some very knotty problem in theology.

Meanwhile his other hand sought for the tail and grasped it. It is here that a lamb carries the secret of its well-being.

I do not imply that one must take notice of how it carries its tail. One must not expect it to hold it stiff and erect — defiant, as a rough-haired terrier carries his, or insultingly bare, as does a billy-goat.

But I learned that if the tail be fat and well-nourished, then the rest of the lamb will tally with it. The tail is the index to the lamb. If the steering-gear be right, you needn't worry about the bow.

Even so Dick's hand felt the tail of each beast. Then a sigh escaped him, and he gave a slight shake of his head. This last movement was intended to convey to Alan and Joe, who were watching him keenly, that he was "not ower-pleased wi' t' lambs." It was a gesture intended to keep down prices. The brothers hardly said a word, but they made great inroads into their stock of tobacco.

★　★　★

Finally, after all had been examined — some having been faintly praised, others depreciated — Dick climbed out of the pen. The battle of prices was about to begin in real earnest.

My impressions are that in buying and selling lambs there are ten rounds. In this contest each round commenced with Dick asking Joe what he thinks they are worth (one must never on any account ask the price direct — this is fatal to the lamb's life). Each round closed with Dick saying what *he* thinks they are worth, and Joe saying in a hurt tone, as though he were wounded to the depths of his being, "I can't let 'em go at that, Dick." As the opposing forces grew a little tired of mere "footwork," then each side tried a little "infighting," and, as a result, prices on each side tended to be modified. Each party, so to speak, retired to his corner, the one offering a little more, and the other pondering as to whether he could let them go. The final bout was usually a compromise, and it was only when Dick and Joe appeared to have reached the limit of concessions that I ventured to "butt in."

"How do you stand now?" I asked.

"There's nine bob atween us," answered Joe.

"That's a matter of eighteen-pence a lamb," I said looking at the six bleaters in the pen.

Neither bargainer appeared as though he would budge an inch nor yield a halfpenny.

Joe leaned up against the pen, smoking his pipe, giving all his answers in the same way. He never looked directly at Dick, but shook his head and gazed intently at the horizon of the hills. Alan also did not speak, but when Joe negatived an offer, he just raised his cap and scratched the top of his head.

This gave an impersonal touch to the haggling. Joe was selling neither for friendship nor with meanness. It was strictly business, and personal relationship did not come into it.

Then Dick picked up his stick and walked toward the gate that led from the farm.

"Nothing doing," I whispered to Alan, but he gave me a wink, and I noticed, too, that Joe had not moved from the pen.

Dick reached the gate, but did not walk through it. He turned and made another offer to Joe, and, as the latter considered it, walked back towards him. As a matter of fact, though that gate was only a few yards distant, Dick did not reach it for nearly an hour!

Each time that he neared it he turned round, and either he or Joe said, "I'll tell ye what I'll do, I'll take —"

So, like a shuttle, Dick moved between the pen and the gate.

"Why don't you split the nine bob?" I asked at last in sheer desperation.

As I said this Dick had his hand on the gate, but at the brilliance of my suggestion and the depth of original thinking which it displayed, he once more turned back and said hopefully —

"What do ye say to that, Joe?"

Then Joe came suddenly to life. He knocked the ashes out of his pipe (Alan, I noticed, did the same), deliberately spat on the ground, raised his cap, rubbed the back of his head, grasped the buyer's hand and gave it a resounding smack, palm meeting palm, and thus clenched the bargain.

"They're yours," he said decisively.

CHAPTER
SEVENTEEN

The Phantom Swimmer

FEBRUARY

The day was beautifully fine. Every field was flooded with sunshine, pale as yet, but still holding out to the world a promise of warmer days. The tops of the trees swayed gently in the breeze, shaking their heads at the sunlight as though they knew that he was a seducer, and that Winter might still spring upon them.

On all sides, however, there were evidences that the sound sleep of the dark months was not so deep. Up in

an elm a thrush poured out a full-throated song: at the back of his mind was the vision of a cosy nest in which would lie four blue-green speckled eggs. This was enough to make any bird sing. The lark quivered aloft, and his song must have penetrated to the depths of burrow and dark retreats, touching all sleepers with a restlessness which made them turn in their beds of moss and leaves and go to sleep again less soundly.

In the tops of the elms the rooks' clamour announced the coming of a new interest. I could see them inspecting the nests which have had such a buffeting in January gales.

As Raq and I entered the low-lying fields, I saw that the plover's plumage had taken on a new neatness, a new sleekness. Gone was the lustreless tone of December. Ivory and white glistened with brilliantine softness. Crests, too, were in evidence, and a new spirit of pugnacity manifested itself. I saw a pair of birds suddenly "square up" to each other. No combatants seem to observe more scrupulously "Queensberry rules" than do these pied rivals. There is a certain etiquette of the boxing-ring which is never overlooked. Both birds advanced, and as they stood opposite each other, they bowed with courtesy and grace, their bills and heads curving towards the grass. Then, having shaken hands so to speak, the gong sounded. For a moment beaks and wings whirled and jabbed without doing any serious damage. The next moment peace reigned again. Probably it was an outlet for the new energy which bubbled in their veins.

144

By the side of a distant hedge Raq drew my attention to a lordly cock pheasant who stalked along with all the pomp of royalty. He walked as though he were conferring a favour on the earth by placing his feet upon it. Once he gave forth a raucous challenge. Perhaps it was a reminder to all sportsmen that a truce should be proclaimed now that Spring was in the making.

★　★　★

In one of the fields I came across the dog sniffing at something. I found two corpses awaiting me — one a rat — at least, all that was left of it; the other was the scarred remains of a mole. Both of them had been dead some hours. I wished that Jerry had been with me, so that he might have described just what had happened. Then I lifted up "the little gentleman in velvet," and saw that his spade-like feet were covered with blood and rat hair. Things then became plainer to me.

I looked around and saw that the mole had been busy hunting for worms. Here and there were piles of freshly-turned-up earth — mounds which spoke of his restless energy, and which also told of the mighty appetite which hounds on this little velvet barrel.

Evidently he had come to the surface at the very moment when the rat had been on his nightly prowl — probably after bad luck in hunting and possessed by a ravenous hunger. Perchance the rat had heard the little burrower in his tunnel below-ground. He had brought ears and nose into full play, and knew to an inch where the soft miner worked. The rat had decided to wait, for he believed that the mole would break the surface of the ground.

I should like to have seen him sitting there with every muscle coiled up like a spring, with whiskers twitching and eyes blazing, waiting for the first sign of his underground victim.

At last, as the mole appeared, with a bound the rat pounced on him. He thought it was going to be an easy win — one quick nip with chisel-like teeth at the base of the skull, and then — oh, joy!

But in the darkness the rodent missed the vital spot by a fraction of an inch, and this was bad for the rat. For the mole turned, and with the fury of a badger dug his feet into the soft underparts of the rat. No unyielding earth met those clawed spades, but warm tender flesh, and before such an onslaught even thick leather would have split. With a shriek of pain the rat bit deeper — it was his last effort — the next moment he was disembowelled.

Then quiet night once more resumed her sway, and the stars looked down upon the pitiful remains of the two combatants — the one with his spinal column severed; the other, a mere dilapidated shell.

As Raq looked up at me with disgust written on his face, I said, "That's the world, the world of tooth and claw which lies hidden in your master and every mother's son of us. And every time I'm kind to you is really a miracle — so don't you forget it, old man," I added, as I patted him affectionately. He gave my hand a quick moist lick, which I understood to mean, "And don't forget that there's other things in us dogs besides bite and fight, master," and then, giving me a knowing look, he went on with his hunting.

★　★　★

In the afternoon we came to the river. The floods had settled, and the river was almost at normal level. Once more the shingle-beds fringed the clear stream, every stone polished by the mad rush of the flood waters. Only the muddy twigs and grass, caught in the branches of alder and willow, spoke of the great yellow tides which had swirled and swished through them.

I kept the dog to heel, for I was anxious to see any heron that might be fishing some quiet pool. I love to see him standing on one leg with all the gravity of an old-time village schoolmaster.

We came at last to where the river swims smoothly over a gravel bed, and then falls over the rocks into a deep pool.

We crept along the fringe of the waters, and I peeped over the edge. For some time I noticed nothing. The cliffs rose sheer out of the dark green water, which, after being churned up by its fall, levelled itself out into a placid sheet. The pinetrees mirrored their slimness in it and the sky overhead reflected itself in patches of blue.

At the far end the gorge narrowed, and big rocks did their best to hold back the pool, which eluded their grasp by a fine spurt of speed.

The dog, who had remained motionless by my side (for he senses those times when stealth and quietness are necessary), suddenly lifted his nose in the air. I never neglect such an action, for I know that some wandering air-current has brought interesting news. When, though still on his haunches, he deliberately wagged his tail, I looked around me with keener scrutiny.

Below me was a flat rock in shadow which had a commanding view of the pool. It was partly screened by bushes. At first I thought that the rock had its usual appearance. Then, on looking closer, I saw that a man's boots were sticking out beyond the bushes. These I recognized as belonging to Jerry. He was very intent watching the waters below him. So hidden was he that had it not been for Raq's nose I should never have noticed him.

For some time I waited, but as he made no movement, I flicked a small stone so that it fell on the rock beside him. As I did so, I gave the hoot of the brown owl.

The old poacher turned his head without moving his body, and through the bushes saw me peering down at him. He put his finger on his lips to enjoin silence, smiled, and beckoned me to join him, indicating the way by which I was to come.

In a moment or two I crouched beside him.

"Where's your gaff?" I whispered, thinking that he was waiting to invite a salmon to accompany him home.

148

He shook his head and laughed quietly. "Not this time. I'm watching them rocks that shelve down to the water ower yonder — there's an otter somewhere aboot there. I've caught a glimpse of him once. He'll be oot when the sun goes down, I reckon — if he's not gone."

★   ★   ★

All three of us kept our eyes on the shelving rock. Raq sat upright between Jerry and me, alert as either of us. But no sign of life stirred either on or behind the rocks.

A slow fanning movement overhead caused me to look up, and I saw a heron go lazily by. He, not having seen us, commenced to plane downwards towards the rock we were watching. As his feet almost reached the landing-place, he changed his mind, lurched violently to one side, and with a hoarse scream of protest continued his flight down river.

"Oor swimmin' friend's there all right," whispered Jerry. "Reckon that otter bared his teeth at 'Owd Longlegs,' and he didn't think twice of movin' on, did he, eh?"

A moment or two afterwards a couple of mallards, with whistling wings, headed in the heron's direction. As they passed the rock in which we were interested, they, too, swerved and flung themselves higher in the air. I never cease to marvel at this manœuvre, so sudden, so sure, so effective in getting them out of the range of immediate danger.

"Them pair (ye saw that they was mated)," said Jerry in a low voice, "caught a glimpse of the otter too."

Next moment my companion nudged me. Simultaneously I felt Raq stiffen with excitement. I looked at the rock, but saw nothing.

"He's in the pool," said Jerry quietly, "didn't ye see him?"

I shook my head. All I could see was a dimple on the smooth surface that kept expanding into ever-widening circles. The otter must have slipped out and in again whilst my attention was on the ducks. I was determined that he should not be missed a second time, and so kept my eyes glued on the darkening waters.

Suddenly, and almost right beneath us, the smooth shadows were parted, the next moment we saw the

otter draw himself out of the water as slick and quietly as though he were a glass tube.

I shall never forget that thrill. First of all he snuffled and blew the water clear of his nose. I could see the sensitive whiskers sticking out each side of his face, and his eyes appeared to be especially round and luminous.

Jerry put his mouth to my ear. "Look's like a brother o' Ole Bill, don't 'e?" I smiled, for there was a decided similarity to Bairnsfather's hero.

Then I looked at his long powerful body from which the icy water dripped on to the shelf of rock, and when he shook himself the fur round his neck stood out like a coarse ruff.

The next moment the otter slid into the water again. How with such a body he managed to enter so quickly and with no sound of a plunge, I could not understand. One moment he was in full view, the next he was not — the waters had closed silently upon him.

As though "Ole Bill" knew that we were watching, and was determined to give us full value for our money, he again came to the surface. Never have I seen such an exhibition. He turned, squirmed, looped the loop, swam on his side, on his back. Like some mighty eel he twisted, rushed at the rocks with incredible speed, and just as we expected him to dash his brains out, put his head down. Then we saw the tail vanishing down the side of the rock, and immediately afterwards his head appeared in the centre of the pool.

Once again we heard the familiar snuffle, and, as he reared himself in the water, he gave a call not unlike the cluck of a moorhen.

Whether it was myself or Raq who, in our interest and excitement, dislodged a stone which crashed into the water, I cannot say. All I know is that there was the sound of a splash. Simultaneously the figure with the creamy breast sank out of view. Nothing remained but the shadowed pool, the evening breeze stirring the tops of the pines, the rushing of icy water beneath us, and a ripple in the middle of the pool, down the centre of which a phantom swimmer had disappeared.

CHAPTER
EIGHTEEN

The Tired, Soiled Things

OCTOBER

Each house in which I have lived has had an attic. I have a liking for these rooms nearest the sky. As a rule they are irregular in shape, and their sloping ceilings, and windows jutting out with shameless curiosity over the surrounding streets, recall the quaintness of country cottages and the glories of thatched roofs. One feels that just below lie the fields and the lane which leads to the main highway.

To begin with, the attic is a museum, and one comes across the things which have been stored away and almost forgotten.

Over there in the corner stand my fishing-rods. I handle them lovingly. That top joint with its neat splice brings back the murmur of running waters, and of the lordly fish in the duel with which I came off second-best. I can once more hear the scream of the reel, feel the mighty pull on the line, see the top curling into a circle, feel my heart leap into my mouth as a crescent moon leaps high in the air — then Ichabod — a slack line and a broken rod.

By the rod stands an old cricket bat. Every scar and dent speaks of "ducks" and triumphs. I take it up and feel its balance, and it gives back to me the voices of the past — "Well played, sir!" — "Hard luck, old man."

The shadowed part is what we call the "condemned cell." It is occupied, according to the house in which we find ourselves, by various articles of furniture — antiques — deposits and relics of former tenants. That "sofa" in the corner, an upholstered horror in

American cloth, ought to be valuable in time, as it must be the only one of its kind. There is the iron bedstead and straw mattress that *may* be needed, the mammoth cheese dish which never will, and the inevitable mahogany curtain poles.

All these, however, may receive their reprieve when the triennial eviction takes place, unless in a moment of forgetfulness we mistake them for firewood.

But as I rummage about I come across other things too. If the attic is a museum to me, it is used by my wife as the half-way house to the jumble sale. In the other corner, and well screened from casual glances, lies a covered heap of clothing. I am almost in the act of passing on to something more interesting when my eye is caught by a familiar piece of cloth. "So that's where my old suit is," I murmur to myself, and pull out of its hiding-place a beloved pair of baggy trousers and a coat that clings lovingly to my shoulders. Very thoughtfully I rescue it from its death sentence. Then I listen from the top of the stairs to make sure that there is no one in the bedroom, and very quietly I take my old friend and reinstate it in my wardrobe.

"By the way," I say casually a little later to my wife, "where is my old brown suit? I haven't seen it lately, and I'm going out with Raq to-morrow."

She looks at me thoughtfully, carefully, as though weighing up her words.

"Oh, I've put it in the attic, dear, there was so little room in the bedroom."

No more is said, but I know that it was put in the attic so that I should forget its existence. If I had not asked for it in six months — it would have gone to the making of cloth-rugs. The attic is a "forgettery." Within limits, things can be produced if asked for. Then — ?

But as I donned the old suit the next morning, there was only one thing I was sure of — it will find its way to the attic again.

★ ★ ★

How good it was to be out in the fields again, and better still to be out with Raq and Ned as companions. Every now and then Ned would stand still before some lovely bit of colour. Once, before a chestnut tree which glowed with Autumn gold he took off his cap, and I heard him murmur, "Take off thy shoes, for the place whereon thou standest is holy ground," and I knew that he was thinking of the "burning bush."

"It's a wunnerful time o' the year," he said.

I answered nothing at first, knowing that this was but the opening aria, a preamble to the thoughts which the old man sometimes revealed. But as my companion looked at me expectantly, I ventured to say —

"A beautiful but rather sad time, I always think. 'Falling leaf and fading flower — Good-bye to Summer,' I quoted.

Ned gave a slight explosion of disgust.

"That's where the poets have gone wrong," he said, and paused.

Then he raised his arm and swept into its wide circle hills and vale.

"Look around ye," he cried, the lustre of the woods giving him inspiration.

"Look around ye — what is it that ye see? Mournfulness and death? Can ye see any signs o' wreaths or the wearin' o' crêpe?"

He stood and pointed first at the beech, then the elm, and finally our eyes rested on a virginia-creeper that nestled blood red against an old grey building.

"Royal colours," he said; "gold, purple, crimson. Natur' putting out her buntin', as I've 'inted at afore. This is her gala season. She's celebratin' the fulfilment of the promise o' the Spring. The white bridal blossom is a prophecy — to-day sees its realization."

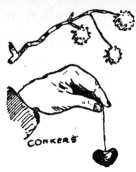

He stooped and picked up from the ground a horse-chestnut — "conkers" I used to call them when a boy. Up the chimney they used to go to harden, and I saw myself with my string of conkers and — I was recalled by Ned saying —

"That's why Natur' is a showin' her flags — the seeds have ripened and most on 'em have bin sown. Her work is done. She goes to her rest like a conqueror."

"But her flags are being lowered," I said.

For answer my companion drew me aside and we stepped over a mossy bank into the wood. No sound of bird or beast broke the silence. The great beeches towered upwards; larches swayed in every little gust of wind; oaks, with gnarled bark, made the aisles in Nature's great cathedral.

Then there came the sound of a sigh, a slight click could be heard, and the next moment a leaf like a golden butterfly was released from a branch — yellow leaves from the elm; saffron, ribbed with brown, from the beech; oak leaves, tough and tawny.

For a second they glided on the wing; now they turned and dived, and the light filtering through the top branches was caught and reflected as they swerved.

156

Now they poised in mid-air as though selecting their landing-place, and descending on the back of some unseen curve, finally rested on the soft carpet of the woods.

" 'Lowerin' their flags,' ye call it," said Ned in a whisper. (Only vandals shout in a wood.) "That is only the beginnin' of another beautiful life."

"It looks very much like the beginning of the end to me," I said, in a tone which I knew would either draw him out or send him into his shell. "As a matter of fact," I went on remorselessly, "we are witnessing the scrapping of so much rubbish. A million energies have quivered in those quiet-lying leaves, a million engines were at work in their construction. Now they are tossed aside as so much waste — and you talk as if they were fluttering to a carnival instead of to their doom."

I expected the old man would flare up at that. But, instead, he looked at me and smiled indulgently.

"Nay," he said, "yer tone belies ye. Ye're just tryin' to pull my leg a bit. Ye canna believe that."

Then, taking my arm, he continued, pointing to the leaves —

"There's no such thing as waste i' the universe. What we call 'waste' is a sign o' ignorance. The world is run on a big borrering and lending principle. Mother Earth advances most o' the goods. The Sun steps in too and lends a 'elpin' hand."

' "Earth to earth and ashes to ashes," ' I quoted.

"That's it noo," said Ned appreciatively. "That body o' yourn is made up o' common clay, whatever there is in it comes oot o' t' earth. It's all bin lent to ye — finally t' mortgage is called in."

We were quiet for a few moments. There was a solemnity about the way he put things, even though there ran through it a lightsome touch.

"And it's the same wi' a leaf," he continued. "Them little butterflies lyin' there'll be caught up i' the first gale which blows. They'll have the maddest gambol o' their lives, o'er hill and glen, o'er moor and fen, till they sink doon and —"

"Rot," I said.

Ned glared at me, and I hastened to change my monosyllable to "Hand in their borrowings."

He nodded, and continued —

"And where they give back what's bin lent 'em will come up the cowslip or the harebell."

"The foxglove and the bee-orchis," I whispered.

"Coloured and made strong by the dust o' the past. No longer dead, but surgin' and swayin' wi' new life. Fer Natur' lays by her tired, soiled things, her used-up things, and they come up fresh agen in other forms."

We left the wood behind us and tramped on in unbroken silence. At last I said —

"And the life that was in the leaf — where does that go?"

"Resides in the tree surely — stored up till the Spring," he answered.

"And the life in the plant that dies with the first nip of the frost — where does that go? You've only accounted for the materials," I persisted.

"That's somethin' that all yer science and chemistry can't answer for sartain," said Ned slowly. "Only living things can tak' up these dead elements and transform 'em into somethin' new. Mebbe it sinks back into the great Lender Hisself." Here he stood still and said quietly: "Shall He make atoms to persist, and leave life to trickle into the void, to waste? It's onthinkable that He should look after the house and fergit the more valuable tenant."

"Unthinkable," I echoed, as we parted.

★　★　★

As we passed through the village I called in to see Sally Stordy for a moment. She was busy with some sewing or other.

As I entered I heard her voice raised in argument, and I saw Billy, one of her boys, standing rather tearfully near to her.

"Says as 'ow 'e wants a new pair o' trousers, and not these," said Sally to me, holding up a patched corduroy pair for me to see, and thus giving me a clue to the domestic trouble.

"I've never 'ad a new pair but once," said Billy. "I've allus got to wear oot oor Jimmy's."

"And Jimmy," said Sally, "what does 'e get? Does 'e have new uns, or do I make his feyther's fit him?

"And what do you do with yours, sir?" she said, turning to me and hoping to find help in my answer. "Where do they go to?"

"The attic," I replied promptly. "And where do Billy's go when he's done with them?"

"There ain't anything to do owt with, when 'e's done wi' 'em," she said significantly. "As far as I can mak' oot, 'e leaves most on 'em on barbed wire and tops o' trees. If there's owt, it ends up as a floor-cloth or kindlin'," she said, pointing to the fire. "There's no waste i' this hoose."

I left for home, and Sally went to feed her hens and pig.

And so I tramped homewards with the vision in my mind of how things are used up. Clothes are passed on from father to child, and from child to smaller child. The hens knead up the fragments into eggs, and the sows churn up the swill-tub into tasty rashers. There is very little wasted in the country.

CHAPTER
NINETEEN

The Sleepers

DECEMBER

December! How splendidly and appropriately this twelfth month is named. August suggests fullness and satisfaction. Then September steals upon us, and there is a suggestion even in the sound of the name of something drowsy, as though the eye-lids were closing. October finds those eye-lids lying quietly closed, undisturbed, unruffled; whilst November is a lullaby distilled into a name. Then December, and peaceful sleep. The word is indicative of what is taking place in the world of field and wood. In hedges and walls, bushes and banks, life is at ebb tide.

I felt this as Raq and I tramped over sodden moors. The gale had blown itself out, leaving a trail of wreckage in its track. Wild life still hid itself in its retreats, only venturing forth to find some snack of food which would help it to face the long night. Now eventide was at hand. Light greyness was merging itself into dark dusk, and over hill and glen, spinney and marsh, a solemn stillness reigned.

Raq and I sat on a stile for a few moments listening to the sounds which only enhanced that stillness. Up in a bare elm a thrush quietly warbled its winter litany. Not full-throated was his song, nor disconnected, as in Spring; but low and melodious, as though he did not wish to disturb a tranquil world. He sang of past joys, and the spirit of reminiscence veiled all harshness and all the flaunting challenge of former days.

Now the lamps glowed in the farmsteads and cottages — not the glare that appears in town houses, but tender yellow glows that welcomed home the tired workers of the field. On the hearth the oak log gleamed red, or the pine branch filled the cosy room with an incense all its own.

Down in those farmsteads, too, were the sounds of peace and content. The stables listened to the steady crunch of the horses. Now and then a pig squealed out a protest as its neighbour tried to squeeze into a warmer corner — a squeal that lost itself in a deeper snore.

From the stacks a rustle in the dry sheaves told of the activities of the long-tailed ones. It was the only sound of virile life to be heard.

Towards a light that twinkled between the bare boughs of an orchard a figure walked. It was John, the keeper, and I hailed him.

"Enjoyin' the quiet?" he asked, as he came up to me. I nodded.

"This is a real rest cure. I'm feeling the silence," I said.

162

★ ★ ★

For a few moments we stood quite still. From a distant wood there floated a raucous call.

"There's a pheasant off to roost," said John. "I allus think the noisy beggars shout out that they're goin' into the tops o' the pines so as to let t' fox know as it's no use tryin' to foller 'em. Sleepin' time fer many is huntin' time fer others, ye know."

"The wonder to me is," I said, "that the birds, when they are once asleep, don't fall off their perches. It must be a ticklish thing to hold on to a branch and to keep your balance when you are dreaming."

John did not answer for a moment, and then said:

"Have you ever noticed a hen's leg when it's walking? If ye have, ye'll a noticed how that every time it takes a step its three toes spread oot when it treads on the ground."

"That's true," I murmured.

"But," said the keeper, "as soon as it lifts its foot off t' ground, them three toes close like an umbrella and bend round in a kind o' grip. Ye've noticed that, too, I reckon?"

I answered nothing, as I had not really observed the way a hen walks. But when John mentioned it, then I recognized his apt description.

"Well," continued the keeper, "as soon as a perchin' bird alights on a branch it grips it with its toes, and as soon as it crouches down ovver its legs Nature locks 'em sure and tight in that position."

163

"So it can go to sleep and can't fall off its roost," I said.

"It can't fall off," echoed John. "But as soon as it rises ready to fly down, the risin' up turns the lock back agin — see?"

★ ★ ★

We walked on together towards his cottage.

"Talkin' o' sleep," John continued, "have ye any idea of how wild Natur' tak's its rest?"

I had to confess that on the whole I had never given the subject much consideration. That birds usually put their heads under their wings, and that rabbits and foxes crept into dark holes, was about the extent of my knowledge. But when John asked his question I at once saw that investigation might prove interesting. So I said:

"Where do the birds sleep, especially at this time of the year?"

For answer John turned aside to one of his out-buildings which was covered with ivy and gave the climbing leaves a few vigorous hits with his ash stick.

164

Immediately there was a fluttering and a scurry, and a score of startled birds vanished into the dusk.

"That's where the sparrows sleep anyway," he said.

And even as he spoke there came from the wood the long quavering "Hoo, hoo, hooter, hoo" of the brown owl.

"I'll bet that old night-prowler knows every inch o' this ivy," he said.

"Why?" I asked, in order to draw him out. "It's not thick enough for him to sleep in."

"It's a happy huntin' ground fer 'im, I reckon. I wasn't thinkin' of it as a roostin' place. Every night," he continued, "especially when mice proves scarce, he comes round here and sits up on that chimney there. Like a carved image he sits, his big eyes on the ivy and his ears listenin' fer the slightest rustle amongst t' leaves. Then, without a ripple in the air, he skims alongside the wall."

"Hooting?" I asked.

"Not allus," answered my companion. "Sometimes he sees the sparrows hunched up in the climbin' branches and then he just nips 'em oot. Other times sees him sort o' disturbin' the outside leaves wi' the tip of his wings — brushin' against 'em like a brown ghost. Then, if he finds nowt, he'll turn and send a cold shiver through every dozin' sparrer by soundin' his quaverin' call. The very hoot must sound to 'em like the waves o' death, and hardly knowin' what they does, they come oot o' their refuge. Feathers, bones, and all, vanish down that girt gullet."

★   ★   ★

Leaving the ivy-covered building, John led me towards his sty. We could hear his bacon-in-the-making lying in blissful ignorance that one day they would swing from the dark rafters of his cottage.

Under the tiles near the ridge of the roof was a small hole, and he told me that it led to a very snug cavity.

"Them pigs acts as central heatin' fer it," he said with a smile, and, giving me a lift, for a fraction of a second I flashed a torchlight in it.

"What do ye see?" asked John.

"About seven or eight Jenny-wrens all bunched up together," I replied.

"That's 'ow that little lot keep warm i' winter nights," he said. "Other wrens, o' course, may not have so snug a hole, but they generally manage to find a bedroom in some old rotten stump or even in some overhanging bank."

As we walked towards John's cottage I said to him:

"Quite a lot of people still think that the Jenny-wren is the mate of Cock-robin."

"Aye," said John. "It's to do wi' that nursery yarn that was told to us when we were childer. But it's only in imagination that these two ever go aboot together. 'Twould be scand'lous, wouldn't it?"

Just before we entered he stopped.

"O' course, ye know, there's all the elements fer a yarn like that to be true if they were human bein's and not birds."

"What do you mean by that?" I asked, as John took a big yard brush and cleaned his boots.

"Well," he said, leaning on the handle of the brush, "we find a good number o' wrens' nests which are never used fer layin' the eggs in even in the nestin' season, and they do say as 'ow the cock builds some on 'em. Ever heard the Jenny-wren let loose her tongue at ye and give ye a bit o' her mind?"

"Often," I answered.

"Well," John continued, but lowering his voice so that those in the cottage might not catch his words, "if ye lived wi' a shrew like yon, I reckon ye would build a sort o' retreat where ye could get a bit o' quiet."

"And how does that fit in with the nursery yarn about the robin?" I asked.

"Oh," laughed John at his own nonsense, "p'r'aps he stayed away so long after a particler bad attack that she thought he'd deserted her, so sought to vary the monotony by takin' up wi' Cock-robin.

"As a matter o' fact," he said as we entered the house, "those extra nests are often used i' the winter by

167

them little Jinnies. If ye'll examine 'em carefully ye'll see that Natur' has made 'em so that they can pack themselves in tight and snug. Ye can't imagine thrushes and blackies crowdin' six or seven in a hole, can ye?"

I must have looked as though I saw no reason why they too should not enjoy community warmth, for the keeper added:

"What ud they do wi' their tails? They can't fold 'em up, and both them birds are rather particler aboot their appearance. But the wren has little use fer a tail. She only hops from one branch to another, so she's reduced it to vanishin' point. And so i' them nests they roost, body to body, and through its tiny door, Jack Frost can't enter."

★   ★   ★

After having the cup that cheers, Raq and I departed. The moon had risen and was bathing the slumbering land in silver. How beautiful the silent wood gleamed in the pale blue light. Every bare patch of ground caught the shadows of the bare branches; its bareness now chased with the delicate filigree work of fantastic patterns.

I stood and gazed at the trees, for they too were asleep. Where the light was strongest I could see the buds formed in the strength of last summer's sunshine. They too were snug in their tightly-fitting casing, and inside that protecting jacket the leaves were taking their beauty sleep before quivering with a thousand energies when the lengthening days should begin to dawn.

Underneath my feet I knew were myriads of seeds — condensed and compressed tabloids of life. They lay secure in the warm arms of Mother Earth waiting for the renaissance of Spring.

In the banks and holes of the trees slept the dormice, hedgehogs, frogs, snails. Perchance the squirrel lay in that dark nest at the fork of the elm branches with his long tail keeping his tender nose warm.

Yes! A sleeping world that would in a few months rouse itself, and like a child at morn come forth with laughing eyes and a beauty distilled from the shadows of the night.

CHAPTER
TWENTY

Nature's Insurance

MARCH

Two or three fields away I could hear the laughing voices of children, and hurrying across the peewit-guarded lands, I came across Jerry and Ned. Jerry was cutting down "palm" and giving the branches to the youngsters for decorating the village church.

Ned, I thought, looked on rather disapprovingly. He hates cutting flowers or stripping trees of their glory — "it's a kind o' murder," he says.

When the children had departed, we all three stood and paid homage to the branches clothed in silver velvet and golden filigree. They brought to my mind the Poet Laureate's beautiful words, and I quoted them knowing it would please Ned —

The woodland willow stands, a lonely bush
Of nebulous gold.
There the spring goddess cowers in faint attire
Of frightened fire.

"Neboolus gold — frightened fire," repeated Ned with shining eyes; "that just aboot hits it off."

While the old postman was saying over to himself the phrases that he so much relished, Jerry wandered down the hedge. I saw him standing before a small tree, and the next moment he called out to Ned to come and have a look.

We found ourselves gazing at another willow, but no golden globes adorned its bare branches. Instead, narrow, grey-green catkins looked out demurely on the Spring morning.

"Is this another kind o' willer, fer there's no palm on't?" asked Jerry, pointing to the bush.

Ned shook his head.

"That's *Mr.* Willow," said Ned, looking back at the tree from which the children had received their gold and silver bunches, "and this is *Mrs.* Willow. Ye know, both on ye, I reckon, that there's male and female in the plant world just as there is male and female in animals."

Jerry made a gesture which conveyed surprise and wonder, and this encouraged the old man to proceed.

"Sometimes," he continued, "ye find the male and female flowers growin' on t' same branch. In the willers they are different trees. The gold un's the male."

"They haven't far to look fer one another, then," said Jerry, with a smile.

Ned glowered at Jerry for a moment, and I nudged him to be quiet. Anything approaching levity, I knew, would make the old man close up as tightly as an oyster.

"Go on, Ned," I said soothingly; "tell us some more."

"If ye want to see what I mean," said he, "look roond fer some hazel catkins. Ye'll find 'em in that spinney yonder. Ye'll not only see the golden 'lambs' tails,' but ye'll come across on t' same branch some little flowers like a fairy brush — them's the females, and the swingin' catkins are the males."

He was quiet for a moment, and then said, "A puff o' wind — a shower o' gold from the shakin' tails — millions o' grains floatin' in the air — most on 'em lost except one or two that settles on the fairy brush — and where they've settled, a little bunch o' nuts in the Autumn."

"Fine," said Jerry appreciatively, and I saw by the look Ned gave him that the poacher had more than made up for his former lightsome remark.

"And millions of grains of life-dust will be wasted?" I asked.

Ned nodded. "If the male flower were mean, and only made a few grains, ye see, they might never find the female flower. But he smothers the air wi' 'em so that some on 'em must find their target. Natur," concluded Ned as he left us, "allus leaves a margin. She's prodigal where life is consarned."

★ ★ ★

Jerry and I moved on towards the spinney which Ned had indicated. We found a few hazel bushes, and after examining them and confirming Ned's statements, Jerry said to me —

"There's summat farther on there that ye ought to see — but put a leash on the dog so as not to disturb it."

After walking for a hundred yards or so, my companion halted before a large clump of hazels, and motioned me to go in carefully.

I could see at a glance that the bare branches held nothing of interest, so I scrutinized the ground. For a long time all that I could see was a carpet of moist beech leaves, with here and there a bit of dark brown withered bracken.

I looked back at Jerry, and as I moved towards the left he said quietly, "Ye're gettin' warmer now."

This time I quartered the ground with my glance, scrutinizing first the leaves which lay at my feet. Then, about six feet away, I suddenly espied two bright dark eyes, motionless, expressionless. As though a puzzle picture began to loom up from amongst a tangle of roots, stems, and grasses, so I traced the rounded head of a wild duck as it curved down towards a brown back beautifully pencilled with dark markings.

She was sitting on a nest the edge of which exactly matched her surroundings in colour. Duck, nest, and environment were a symphony in brown. I had only to glance away for a moment to lose sight of them.

I crept nearer to her. She never moved a muscle. What strength of will or instinct she must have had to sit like a carved statue whilst an enemy walked so close to her treasures!

173

Then, unfortunately, as I backed away, thinking that I would leave her to reign in solitary grandeur, I stumbled over a concealed root.

There was a hasty rush by the startled bird from the nest. The next moment she appeared a few yards from me as a bruised thing with a broken wing, whilst her eyes looked expectantly at me, hoping that I should give chase — a trick that had been handed down to her through centuries of duckdom.

Seeing that I refused to be drawn, she hobbled away, and a moment or two later we heard her wings whistling over the tops of the trees.

"That's a bit of real artistry," I said to Jerry, as we both examined the nest.

"Thirteen eggs," said Jerry, pushing aside the down at the edges of the nest. "I wonder how many on 'em 'll ever grow up."

$\star$　$\star$　$\star$

As we retraced our steps through the wood, the old poacher said, "I reckon that if she rears a couple on 'em it 'll be aboot the limit."

"Two out of thirteen?" I said, rather incredulously.

Jerry nodded. "That's why she lays thirteen or more," answered my companion; "it's Ned's story o' Natur' allus allowin' a margin all ovver agin. Mind ye," said he, after a moment, "I don't say as 'ow she thinks it all oot, but instinct makes her hatch oot more'n ever'll grow up."

174

"Why?" I asked, hoping to draw out some reminiscence. "What perils have the ducklings to face? They can swim and dive as soon as they are dry and out of the shell."

We were on the edge of the wood at the time, and Jerry, pointing to the river, asked me how far it was from the wood.

"I should say it was about half a mile," I answered.

"Well, then," Jerry continued, "try and think o' them youngsters as soon as they are oot o' t' shell. The old duck's first job is to get 'em doon to t' river. They all set off — the young uns followin' 'er, peepin' and cheepin' like young canaries. They meet wi' all sorts o' adventures. There are holes i' the ground, and mebbe a little un falls in't. If he can get hissel' oot, well and good. If he can't, then he stays there. The owd duck won't lift him oot.

"She leads 'em doon a drain, mebbe, that runs into a dyke. What hides in the holes o' that drain?"

"Rats," I said.

Jerry nodded. "An' as the little uns foller their mother the weakest is at the end o' t' line. He mebbe stumbles ovver a stone, lies ovverturned on his back fer a minnit, and gives his shrill little cry o' fear. But he never gives another, though the mother duck stops and

175

looks roond to see what's t' matter. She sees nowt wrang, fer a rat has nipped it i' the back o' t' neck and dragged it up a hole. That's two on 'em vanished."

"She'll be all right, though, when she gets to the open ground," I said, pointing to the corner of the spinney.

Jerry nodded. "All reet so long as no sparrer-hawk is on t' watch. A duck on t' land is aboot as awkord as a coo i' thick mud — she's not in her nateral element."

"Well," I said, "with any luck she'll still have eleven youngsters to carry on with when she reaches the river."

Jerry did not say anything for some moments, and we walked towards the river itself. Finally we reached a place where the current was sluggish and where the reeds were already beginning to show their Spring colours.

★ ★ ★

"Ye see that bit o' slow water there," said he, pointing to a still pool which lay at our feet. "I was sittin' here one day last Spring, and there, amongst t' reeds, I saw a big pike."

"He's a shark of the fresh water," I interpolated.

MALLARD

"A real un an' all," Jerry went on. "He was aboot ten pun if an ounce. He lay there amongst t' weeds like a striped shadder o' doom. So I says to mysen, 'I'll have ye oot o' that, ye beggar.' So I got some wire oot o' my pocket —"

"You always keep that on you for mending purposes, I suppose," I said with a smile.

"Wi' a bit o' wire, a bit o' string, a knife, and a half-a-croon, ye can face t' world," said he, with a grin.

"Well, as I was sayin'," Jerry went on, "I soon 'ad a runnin' noose made. Then I cut doon a willer stick, tied t' wire on t' end on't, and then" — (here Jerry suited the action to the word) — "I gently lowered it till I'd got his tail inside t' noose."

Jerry then gave a quick pull, a dexterous twist of the wrist, a reaching down as he lifted the big brute out of the water, and in imagination I could see it lying stretched out on the rock.

"I gave him a knock on t' head with a stone, and that finished his day's work. But when I oppened him oot" — (here Jerry looked at me significantly) — "there were two young ducklin's inside o' him. That's why Natur' allus leaves a margin for eventooalities."

★   ★   ★

"I have often wondered," I said to my companion as we walked along the bank, "whether animals grieve?"

"Some do, and most don't," answered he promptly. "It wouldn't be 'ardly fair to mak' a world where losses were allus happenin', if the losers had the power o' grievin' much, would it? Don't ye worry yesen ovver that side o' t' question, fer ye're not dealin' wi' human bein's. If all her ducklin's went west, t' owd duck 'ud be more anxious to raise another brood as quick as she could, than spend time in pipin' her eye, I can tell ye."

CHAPTER
TWENTY-ONE

The Revelations
of Raq

I am a Spaniel, and I would rather be that kind of a dog than any other in the world. I once overheard my master say, "There is no more intelligent or lovable beast than a Spaniel." That is why I am so content.

Many people say that animals cannot think or reason. That is why I am putting down a few of my thoughts on paper.

To begin with, I was born in a big box, and though I do not remember a great deal about it, yet some things do come back to me.

I was brought into the world blind, but I could wriggle about from the first minute. Perhaps that is why I was born with my eyes shut — so that I shouldn't wander very far from the warm nest.

I knew that I was not the only one, for I could hear other little squeaks and feel other wrigglers roll on to me. The only things that I was really conscious of were: firstly, a big warmth that it was jolly to be beside, secondly, a big hole in my inside which this "big warmth" had the means of filling.

The "big warmth," of course, was my mother, and I cannot describe how beautiful was the milk she gave to us.

Though I could not see, yet I could smell, and that is how I used to nose my way to the source of supply. I always fought for the same place at meal-times. The best place was nearest to our mother's head, and the weakest of my brothers and sisters always got pushed lower down to the other end. I believe those ill-behaved creatures which "humans" call pigs refer to the weakest as the "runt" or the "wreklin" — at least I have heard farmers refer to them as such.

It was a great day for me when my eyes were opened. I believe I was nine days old at the time. I remember it because somebody came and picked me up, and I felt the first touch of fingers and the cold chill of the outside air.

But as soon as I was back again in the box my mother licked me all over. This was not because I was dirty, but because she said that it was dog's custom never to let any human scent remain on young dogs. She told us that puppies themselves had a scent, but that if they lay still it grew very faint, and so any passing enemy went by without doing any harm.

When we asked her why we had a scent at all, she told us that we should learn the reason fully when we were older. Of course I now know that it is one of the ways whereby dogs recognize one another. With a good breeze blowing I can smell one of my own friends quite a field away.

★ ★ ★

As we grew older, so we were able to move our legs about and see better. At first we could only distinguish light from shade. Then we could see things that moved. Finally we were able to distinguish everything that was near at hand.

When this time arrived, then our mother used to encourage us to play and tumble about together. She brought to us a piece of rag and we used to play tug-of-war. Then we had mimic battles amongst ourselves, and sometimes the play would get rather rough. Then sometimes our mother would growl out her displeasure, and I have seen her nip one of my brothers with her teeth.

"You'll need all your strength in the big outside world," she used to say. "So play on. You will find out what you can and what you can't do. As it is all in fun and nothing depends on it, failures don't matter. But in the big world outside, failure oftentimes means suffering and death." So we used to struggle and play for hours on end, and I could feel my soft flesh turning into muscle and my limbs getting bigger and more firmly set.

Now that I am older, I can see the value of these play-hours. I did not know what I was doing at the time, but now I am grown up I do in the emergency what I have learnt in fun — and do it with confidence.

Just take, for instance, that greyhound who lives down the road. When he was a puppy I have seen him chasing his brothers and sisters in circles.

That is how he learnt to swerve and turn quickly, and now when he hunts the quick-footed hare, he knows not only how to turn, but what speed in turning is safe.

Of course, we were taught other things. When we went for a walk with our mother, she used to put her nose deep down into things which were harmless, and we used to smell it after her, and store up the smell in our brains. Humans store up all kinds of things in their minds. They know their houses by their numbers or names. We know them by their smells.

But if a thing were harmful, our mother would put her nose down to it, then she would lift her head and walk away. Sometimes her tail would stop wagging, and then we knew that what she had found was very injurious. Human beings are eye-minded and ear-minded, but we dogs are nose-minded. We live in a world chiefly of scents and smells. When we meet one another we do not say, as my master does, "How do you do?" or talk about the weather. We ask, "Good scenting?"; and if the scent is in the air, we raise our noses, if strong on the ground, we turn our muzzles downward.

★   ★   ★

As soon as ever we could trot about as puppies, our first instinct was to follow the big one that protected and fed us. That is why we like to attach ourselves to human beings. Perhaps there is a deeper reason too, for I remember my mother telling us that thousands of years ago all dogs lived like wolves in packs, and followed a trusted leader. I believe she said that at one time we were wolves, but had developed into something better — just as my master's ancestors were once monkeys, and now he is a man.

But the other reason why we love human beings is because we do not like being alone. We are not individualists, like cats who live for themselves and themselves alone — selfish spitfires, who love places rather than people, and who only live near to human beings because they find them their food easily. In those far-off days my mother told me that we all lived in packs, and so we have a sociable nature and can enter into family life. That is what makes us such good watch-dogs. We do not bark to keep people awake at nights, but because it is in our nature to warn the whole pack if we think that we scent danger. You have never heard a cat giving the alarm at night. Also, I think, that we are restless at nights because when we were in a wild state our great foe used to prowl about — I mean the leopard, who liked nothing better than a dog for his supper. I have often wondered whether our dislike and suspicion of a cat really grew out of our hatred of the leopard, for this animal is nothing more than a big cat, and belongs to the same family.

★ ★ ★

It was a great day for me when my master came and chose me for his very own. He looked at me and my brothers, and then, picking me up, said, "That's the little beggar I want," and I knew by the very feel of his fingers and the tone in his voice that he loved a dog.

That, by the way, is how we understand most of what humans say — by the tone; not merely by the words. I like my mistress, but she always puzzles me because she issues her commands in different words. My master says "Seek," or "Fetch my slippers," and I know what he means every time. But my mistress says, "Go into the kitchen and bring your master's slippers," or "Your master wants his slippers." Fortunately the word "slippers" is an easy tone to remember, and gives me the clue.

But what a curious new world I had come to, and how quickly I was expected to learn a thousand different details.

I might go down the steps which lead from the kitchen to the garden, but I was not allowed (at least when my master was out) to go upstairs in the house. He used to take me up into his study, and when my mistress was away from home I used to sleep in his bedroom at the foot of his bed. What interested me most was the way he used to take his outer skin off, so that I hardly recognized him except by his scent before he got into bed.

Then I was expected to know whom to bark at and whom to wag my tail at. My mistress scolded me one day for growling at a friend of hers, but I didn't like her at all, and I knew she didn't like dogs, although she tried to pat me.

Once when some visitors came to the front door, I growled at them, and was sent to the kitchen in disgrace. They had a good meal in the dining-room, too, and I heard them laughing and talking. But after they had gone I heard my mistress say, "Weren't they dreadful people?" Now if she disliked them so much, why ever didn't she let me send them away from the door when they first came as I wanted to? These are the sort of things that puzzle me.

If I meet a dog and we are not on good terms, I don't let him come near me. I just show my teeth and put up the fur round my neck. That is generally a good enough warning.

Again, all my food is put on the floor in a basin. But how can I be expected to know that it is the only dish I may touch. There is one wonderful small room, white and clean, with a lot of shelves in it. Oh! what appetizing odours issue from under the doors — stews — gravies — joints. But if I find the door open and some pan or other on the floor, I'm not even allowed to skim the top of it with my tongue — and in dogdom, "Finding's keeping!"

★　★　★

I love my master, but he has such curious ways. People say that animals are "creatures of instinct and habit," and do everything without reason. But just think what funny things he does. Sometimes when he comes to dinner I have heard him say, "Oh! I'm not at all hungry." But he eats his dinner all the same.

Now animals never do that. You never find them eating when they aren't hungry. Human beings eat just because it has become a habit with them. Then they wonder why they don't feel well.

Then as I sit in the dining-room I wonder at the different kinds of food that they mix up together. At first I thought that my master would choose one of the dishes and no more. If he were a dog he would have chosen the meat, and have eaten that and nothing else. But he mixes it with potatoes and sodden cabbage or turnips. Then, on top of it all, he sends down custard and apple-pie, and sometimes he pours coffee on the whole lot. But animals never eat and drink at the same time.

If my master's boy or girl doesn't feel well, he gives them drugs and medicine. I've noticed that he always tries it on them or on my mistress first. That is another thing which proves how unselfish he is. We animals, however, rely on a good starve when we are not well, and drink big draughts of cold water.

Another thing puzzles me. My master is very fond of washing himself. He even uses a flashing knife to one part of his face. But he never thinks of washing his inside as well as his outside. We dogs, however, think even more of that than we do of our skins, and so we drink as much water as we can hold, and whenever we can. I don't think I ever remember seeing my mistress drink any cold water. She always heats it up first, and colours it a dark brown.

★ ★ ★

Talking about being in the dining-room at meal-times reminds me of another thing which took a lot of learning.

Sometimes my master would give me a little piece of meat, and my mistress would say — "You know, dear, you should not feed that dog in here."

I used to think that he looked a bit frightened when she spoke like that, but he soon recovered. I've been with him at all hours of the day and night, and I used to think that he was absolutely fearless. I've seen him playing football, and the way he knocked over big men proves that he has tremendous courage. But a little sentence like that seemed to bowl him over. If he had a tail, I'm sure he would have dropped it between his legs, just as I do when I feel nervous. Why he doesn't use his football strength at such times puzzles me.

Then I've heard my mistress say, "That dog does bolt his food ravenously. I wonder why he eats so badly."

She forgets that it is my nature to eat like that. A cat is a solitary creature and hunts alone. Consequently she can take her kill away to some quiet corner and eat it leisurely. There is no one to share it with her.

But we dogs, being members of a pack, used to bring down the buck or the sheep, and immediately it belonged to us all. Those who could eat quickest got the most. Those who ate slowly, if there were any, went away hungry.

★ ★ ★

The best time of my life is when we go to live in tents. Sometimes my master packs up a small one, and then he and I go off together, eat together, sleep together.

Then it is that he even dresses differently. There is no stiff white collar round his neck. I can't understand why he has this on, for every dog hates a collar — it is the sign of servitude, and my master is no slave. I have even heard him call it a "dog collar," and I know by his tone that he hates it too. Once when it lay on the ground I saw some printing on the inside, so perhaps that is his name and address engraved on it, like some of our collars have. Perhaps, not being able to scent his way, as we can, he easily gets lost in the streets of a big town.

Then when we go off alone, he leaves his heavy boots in the tent, and for hours goes about unshod, even as I do. His hat, too, is put on one side, and he walks about a real man.

But as soon as we get back to town again, all the old things are back again in their places. It is a pity that he is such a creature of habit.

★   ★   ★

Then, too, I've noticed that my mistress has curious ways of dressing. She, too, wears an outer skin like my master, but she moults far oftener. When I compare her with the other women in the streets I notice that she is wearing similar colours and similar shapes. In fact, there is as much sameness in women's skins as in men's, only, as I say, they cast their skins oftener.

This is because they are like dogs, members of a pack, social animals.

You see, in our original state, all wild dogs were brown. Such a colour hid them from their foes. If a striped dog had appeared they would have chased him from the tribe. Why? Because an odd-looking dog would have made the whole pack conspicuous — a prowling leopard would have noticed the striped one, and so the pack would suffer. And so every dog has to be like his neighbour. If he isn't, he suffers.

I suppose that must be why my mistress, along with other members of the herd, all dress alike. The leaders of the pack must meet somewhere and decide what the colour and shape of the new skin is to be. Then the commands are issued. I have noticed that my mistress is continually receiving circulars with colours and patterns of what she calls frocks on them — so these must be the orders issued from headquarters.

Very few indeed dare disobey these commands, for, if any of them dress differently, they are like a striped dog in a pack, and get unwelcome attention. Humans call it "being out of fashion," whatever that may mean.

★　★　★

I went to a show once, and, by the way, got a red ticket — First prize. But all the dogs were amused at the manner of judging. The shape of our heads, length of ears, straightness of legs, clean feet, the way we carried our ears and tail — all these were taken into consideration.

But the real test no one ever called for. The nose is the real test of a dog. We ought to have been made to retrieve something, to find our way back ten or twenty miles from home, to detect the criminal from the law-abiding citizen. Not features, but qualities and virtues, ought to fit us for a prize.

Then there were "little microbes" — I call them: toy-dogs lying on cushions and having great bows of ribbon round their necks. What a disgrace to dogdom! Their bleary, bulgy eyes and snorting snub noses made them good for nothing but a lady's lap — unhealthy little beasts. I dare not allow myself to write down what I think of them.

★   ★   ★

Only one more word will I write. I love being with my master at all times. I have heard him say many times, and I am very proud when he says it, "The more I see of men, the better I love my dog." Whether he takes me in the fields or in the town, it is all the same to me so long as I am with him.

But the best time is when he sits in his study quietly alone. Perhaps he is reading and having a smoke at the same time.

Then I like to draw up near to him and just touch him somewhere. It doesn't matter what part of him I touch, so long as we are in contact.

Then his thoughts run into me, and I think mine do into him. He says he owns me, and so he does. But I own him too.

SIGNED

RAQ
(HIS MARK)

ISIS publish a wide range of books in large print, from fiction to biography. Any suggestions for books you would like to see in large print or audio are always welcome. Please send to the Editorial department at:

ISIS Publishing Ltd.
7 Centremead
Osney Mead
Oxford OX2 0ES
(01865) 250 333

A full list of titles is available free of charge from:
Ulverscroft large print books

(UK)
The Green
Bradgate Road, Anstey
Leicester LE7 7FU
Tel: (0116) 236 4325

(Australia)
P.O Box 953
Crows Nest
NSW 1585
Tel: (02) 9436 2622

(USA)
1881 Ridge Road
P.O Box 1230, West Seneca,
N.Y. 14224-1230
Tel: (716) 674 4270

(Canada)
P.O Box 80038
Burlington
Ontario L7L 6B1
Tel: (905) 637 8734

(New Zealand)
P.O Box 456
Feilding
Tel: (06) 323 6828

Details of **ISIS** complete and unabridged audio books are also available from these offices. Alternatively, contact your local library for details of their collection of **ISIS** large print and unabridged audio books.